JAKARTA INSIDE OUT

DANIEL ZIV

JAKARTA INSIDE OUT

EQUINOX
PUBLISHING
JAKARTA · SINGAPORE

Equinox Publishing (Asia) Pte. Ltd.
PO Box 6179 JKSGN
Jakarta 12062, Indonesia

www.EquinoxPublishing.com

JAKARTA INSIDE OUT
©2002 Daniel Ziv

ISBN 979-95898-7-8

First Equinox Edition 2002

C O N T E N T S

Introduction 8

INTRODUCTION
AND
RULES OF ENGAGEMENT

Most of this book was researched at ground level – hopping buses with street musicians, checking out bad-ass nightclubs, winding through town on motorbike taxis, and pounding the pavement in Chinatown. But right now I'm typing these lines in a high-rise apartment, with a bird's eye view of this crazy city I've grown to love.

Jakarta is not what you'd call a beautiful place. It's a chaotic maze of low-lying slums, gleaming skyscrapers and imposing toll roads, enveloped in a gigantic cloud of pollution and trapped in hopeless gridlock. It often seems a miracle the place keeps ticking at all. But it ticks. Like crazy. If it's sometimes a city in crisis, it's also one of great opportunity. If it's a city of despair, it is at turns one of hope. A constant assault on the senses, it oozes wacky character.

This book is not really a 'guide' to Jakarta. There's no map in here and no sections entitled 'Where to Stay and Eat' or 'How To Get Around'. Rather, it is a snapshot of a 21st-Century Southeast Asian city bursting at the seams but plugging along nonetheless; of ordinary people in their urban landscape; of culture and pop culture.

More than anything else, the book tries to tell the truth about Jakarta. It celebrates its quirky vibe, but confronts the poverty, corruption, sleaze and injustice that are tightly woven into the city's tapestry. Like Jakarta itself, this book is full of idiosyncrasies, inside scoops, strange anecdotes and a whole slew of shameless contradictions.

To pre-empt inevitable gripes about the content and structure of the book, an early defense: Anyone familiar with Indonesia will notice that some of the topics in here are not unique to Jakarta, but characterize the country as a whole. Clove cigarettes, durian and karaoke for instance, are no more 'Jakarta' than they are any other city in Java or Sumatra. But I tried to select topics that define contemporary Jakarta as we experience it. Put another way, could one imagine a Jakarta without the sweet scent of *kretek* cigarettes, the unmistakable odor of durian, or the tacky karaoke tunes drifting out from lounges all over town?

The overlaps and differences between so-called 'Jakarta things' and 'Indonesia things' are actually quite revealing. Oftentimes, Jakarta seems a microcosm of the archipelago as a whole – a fusion of immigrant ethnic groups, traditions and tongues from all over the country. At others, this melting pot, with its peculiarities and knack for reinvention, resembles no other place on earth.

Topics in the book are arranged alphabetically, although some letters are so interesting they've warranted more than one topic and – believe it or not – some letters received none at all. My apologies to fans of the letters F, I, Q, V, X, Y and Z.

I dreamt up this book as a love letter to a city I've been proud to call home for a number of years now. From the very start it has been a great privilege to live in a place blessed with so much human energy and warmth. That said, it is always problematic when a foreigner comments on a place or a people not their own. No matter how much one feels a part of the scene, a foreign lens can distort observations, and interpretations tend to reflect that. There also exists the danger of over-romanticizing the subject, or worse, being condescending.

I'm certainly not immune to these pitfalls, nor would I claim to be an 'insider'. Much about this city still baffles me. I've tried to understand Jakarta from the point of view of its residents, so research meant hanging out with people from all walks of life, hearing their stories and perspectives and taking copious notes.

But I then put my own spin on things because authors, I believe, must offer something of themselves. If my voice is somewhat uneven – at turns harsh, sentimental, cynical, or just plain silly – it is because Jakarta evokes all of these responses. And while trying to be culturally sensitive, I avoided adopting the sort of exaggerated political correctness that obscures flavor, nuance and truth. I'm convinced that to care about something necessitates being honest about it.

My hope is that at the very least, and despite the humorous undertones, certain comments in here will spark a meaningful debate about the civic issues that affect us all. Jakarta possesses many wonderful qualities, qualities of the human soul. Hopefully the reader will discover some of them between these covers.

Daniel Ziv
Jakarta, September 2002
daniel@equinoxpublishing.com

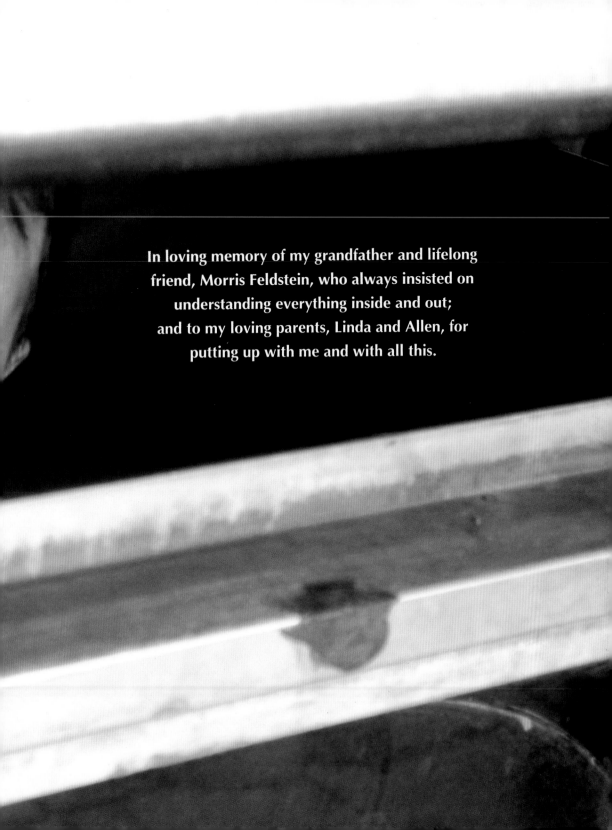

In loving memory of my grandfather and lifelong friend, Morris Feldstein, who always insisted on understanding everything inside and out; and to my loving parents, Linda and Allen, for putting up with me and with all this.

LIKE MOSQUITOES negotiating a bad traffic jam on foot, they weave and buzz with determination from one car window to the next. Overloaded cardboard boxes hang heavily from their necks, they often squat down to rest on the roadside. With cigarettes necessarily close at hand, most smoke like chimneys. These are Jakarta's ubiquitous *asongan*, young men (and sometimes women) that are the local answer to a roadside drive-thru or a highway convenience store.

A typical *asongan* stocks just about anything considered essential on the road. First and foremost: cigarettes, sold either by pack or by individual stick; bottled water; breath mints; tissue packs; shelled or unshelled peanuts; lighters and matches; chocolate bars; gossip tabloids, energy drinks (see 'Krating Daeng' chapter); tofu and chili snacks.

The robust cardboard contraptions (called *'lang'*) that carry an *asongan*'s wares are usually made at home by the vendor himself based on standard size and shape specifications. They cost as little as Rp 15,000 (around $1.50) to produce, meaning *asongan* start-up expenditures are low indeed. *Asongan* must buy their stock in cash from small local agents, and normally pull in a profit of Rp 30,000 (around $3) per day. Most *asongan* work Jakarta's large traffic light intersections, whilst some head out to ply the busy inter-city toll roads.

One of the most lucrative beats for *asongan* is the road out to Puncak. The incredible traffic gridlock there on weekends (see 'Puncak' chapter) means *asongan* enjoy a captive consumer base of thousands of hungry, worn out, and irritable families to serve through tinted, vomit-stained car windows.

THE BRIGHT ORANGE NUISANCE known as the *bajaj* (pronounced "BA-jai") is undoubtedly the cockroach of the automotive world and an element of Jakarta many residents love to hate. These motorized three-wheeled boxes are noisy, belch thick black fumes from their rear ends, veer wildly in their movements and somehow always seem to be in the way. They officially seat two passengers, but have been known to hold a family of four plus three overstuffed shopping bags, one restless goat and two decidedly nervous chickens. Small windows on either side allow for a bit of air to enter – a system hard-core city folks fondly refer to as *AC alam*, or 'natural air-conditioning'. But on a stifling hot day *bajaj* feel like saunas inside; on a rainy day like a steam room. A no-frills, mobile spa! An estimated 20,000 or so zip along Jakarta's side roads and back streets. They get people where they want to go, and are cheap to operate.

The *bajaj* is the curious brainchild of Bajaj Auto Ltd India, and was introduced in Indonesia in 1975 at the behest of then-Jakarta Governor Ali Sadikin (see 'Bang Ali' chapter), who sought an alternative to the motorized, rickshaw-like *helicak*. The buzzing *bajaj* pests were first imported by Indonesian-Chinese businessman Eddy Tansil, who in 1994 was implicated in one of Indonesia's biggest-ever banking scandals. Two years later, Eddy waltzed out of prison after bribing a warden to 'drive him to the doctor', fled to China, and is now the proud owner of a major brewery in Fujian Province. Yeah, Eddy!

A circular spray-painted symbol on the *bajaj*'s door indicates the designated mayoralty within the city where the vehicle is allowed to operate, each mayoralty marked in a different color. Drivers must stick to their area and are prohibited from using many main roads, so *bajaj* routes can be quite circuitous.

In mid-2001, the municipality announced that fume-emitting *bajaj* would gradually be phased out and replaced by a more sophisticated four-wheeled, natural gas-powered *Kancil* ('mouse deer'). Most Jakartans doubt this will really happen, chiefly because the city administration has rarely been known to do anything environmentally friendly. *Bajaj* owner unions have also resisted the move, prefering the current low-cost, low-maintenance vehicles, given that drivers pull in only Rp 30-40,000 (around $3 to $4) on a good day. Sporadic attempts by the government to ban *bajaj*, dating as far back as 1980, cause major fluctuations in the vehicle's market price: the normal value of a good *bajaj* is around $1,500, but when an impending ban is rumored, it can drop to as little as $700. About 1,000 roadside repair shops in Jakarta miraculously revive broken *bajaj* that have long exceeded official shelf life. Through the improvised use of spare parts, like Vespa sparkplugs and retreaded wheels, even the most mangled *bajaj* can normally be fixed in about three hours.

THE GUY CALLING VIRTUALLY all the shots in this city – Jakarta's head honcho – is the all-powerful Governor. Our city has had pretty rotten luck in this field; Jakarta's governors have mostly been colorless ex-military men exhibiting an unfortunate lack of vision and pretty poor job performance.

One man stood out and made his mark on the city, leaving a legacy against which every governor after him has been measured and come up short. Ali Sadikin, nicknamed *Bang* Ali ('Brother Ali'), served the city for eleven eventful, controversial years between 1966 and 1977. Handsome and charismatic, he is widely considered the father of Jakarta development, and the man credited with transforming the capital from a big village into a modern cosmopolitan city.

Bang Ali began his high-profile career as a Major-General in the Indonesian marines, and went on to serve as a cabinet minister. As Jakarta Governor, he was the only senior government official to survive the tumultuous transition between presidents Sukarno and Soeharto. He held on to power despite being a relatively outspoken critic of Soeharto and of the Indonesian military's involvement in politics. He maintains his reformist credentials even today.

Bang Ali was a powerful governor who put his personal stamp on city planning, municipal administration, and the socioeconomic development of Jakarta. Under his watch the capital's administrative machinery was reorganized, master planning for Greater Jakarta was approved, *kampung* (neighborhoods) were fixed up, law enforcement was taken seriously, and local revenue rose sharply. Much of this was possible thanks to a thriving gambling industry, which *Bang* Ali legalized so it could be used to fund city development.

His tenure was marked by new, often iron-fist initiatives: He banned small vendors from operating on footpaths and roads, designating special areas for petty trade; he expelled street beggars and *becak* drivers (see 'Becak' chapter); he essentially legalized prostitution, relocating sex workers to authorized operating venues; he regulated the use and ownership of land and buildings; he put flood prevention measures in place; and he regulated the use of electricity by finally putting an end to illegal tapping.

Such strong-armed policies were not without side effects, and critics accused *Bang* Ali of developing his modern city at the expense of powerless slum-dwellers. But nobody could deny that *Bang* Ali's vision and no-compromise approach altered Jakarta's physical appearance and reinvigorated its character. Perhaps most famously, he is credited for single-handedly livening up the Thamrin boulevard area and kick-starting Jakarta's gambling and entertainment industry. He is also famous for his love of the arts. He established the once-popular art market at Ancol amusement park, and was a founder of the vibrant TIM cultural center (see 'TUK & TIM' chapter).

They sure don't make Governors like they used to.

BECAK

THE THREE-WHEELED pedal-rickshaw known as the *becak* is one of the most colorful and enduring forms of local transport, and still creaks defiantly along Jakarta's narrow back streets. In recent years, with government attempts to ban *becak* from operating in the city, the vehicle and its drivers have become potent symbols of the working class' struggle against oppression at the hands of municipality.

Becak appeared in Dutch-ruled Batavia in the 1930s, and were initially seen as dangerous and unreliable. Although they eventually became popular, they have since frequently been the focus of controversy. *Becak* were first banned from the city's main streets in 1972, and were once described by Jakarta's deputy-governor as "the last example of man exploiting man." They were later confined to tiny back streets, then sporadically banned outright by the authorities. In the 1990s *becak* even became the personal target of President Soeharto, who resented the eyesore, the *becak*'s disruption to traffic flow, and it's supposedly 'primitive' and 'degrading' nature. The erratic municipal bylaws governing *becak* operation have meant that drivers face unemployment at a moment's notice, and thousands have given up and relocated to West or Central Java. But *becak* unions are well organized, and colorful three-wheeled mass-protests have become a common sight along the capital's major thoroughfares. *Becak* are still a popular form of transport at Chinatown's Glodok market, in certain working-class suburbs, and even right outside the glitzy Plaza Indonesia shopping mall in Central Jakarta.

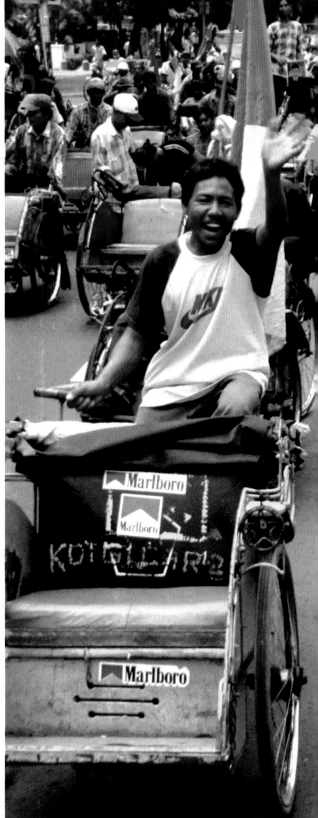

BILLIARDS

FOLKS WILL TELL YOU badminton is the Indonesian national sport, and there's plenty of truth in that. But Jakarta's most popular urban pastime has got to be billiards. Not in the stuffy Western big-tournament sense, but in the "let's-kill-time-while-watching-our-girlfriends-lean-over-for-a-shot-with-their-ass-arched-impossibly-high-in-the-air" sort of way. Yes, billiards in Jakarta is about appraising members of the opposite sex from new and interesting angles, letting off steam with colleagues after work, and sometimes even sinking that Nine Ball into the top left pocket. It is also one of the only sports in Jakarta played equally, and often jointly, by men and women.

Billiard halls are found everywhere in Jakarta – from dimly lit neighborhood shacks with a single, thoroughly abused table, to trendy up-market venues with state-of-the-art equipment. The mother of Jakarta's billiard halls is Bengkel, formerly a hard-core dance club located beneath the city's Semanggi flyover. Here – on what used to be a frenzied trading floor for ecstasy pills during thumping all-night raves – sits a mind-boggling 120-table orgy of billiard activity, one of the largest such halls in Asia. Jakarta's teenagers pack into this place after school, or even skip classes to play here during the day; twentysomethings swamp the venue on weekends, when boyband tunes permeate the air and the waiting list for a table can be an hour long. The 'cool' factor is important here: people look and feel good around a billiard table; in between concentrating on making that perfect shot, they flirt and exchange handphone numbers. Best time to visit is late on a Friday or Saturday night. Climb up to the balcony and take in the sweeping view of the madness below.

JAKARTA HAS NO SINGULAR 'city center', but if it did, it would probably be Blok M – shopping district, entertainment Mecca, restaurant row, and the point where the city's passionately disparate North and South come together. Night and day here offer very different experiences.

The area has been a favorite nocturnal hangout for decades. In the 1980s global kitsch culture was celebrated here at two outrageously popular roller-discos – Lipstick and Happy Day. It was at these venues, and along the adjoining, always-teeming boulevard of Jalan Melawai, that teenagers came of age. Even today, Melawai's streetside *lesehan* ('on-the-floor') snack stalls remain a popular spot for a post-clubbing chill-out.

In the 1990s Japanese karaoke bars, Izakaya-style diners and Japanese specialty supermarkets sprung up all over the few square blocks of nearby Kompleks Blok M. The enclave is nicknamed 'Japan Town', and a stroll here feels a bit like walking through a busy Tokyo neighborhood – tipsy Japanese salarymen and all. Blok M is also home to numerous seedy bars and dance clubs, mostly meat markets for expatriate men on the prowl. The more up-market Jalan Mahakam section of the neighborhood is known for its great restaurants and cafes.

Daytime in Blok M is just as busy, but the emphasis is on shopping. High-end boutiques and salons are tucked away in the leafy streets of the adjacent Kebayoran Baru quarter; middle-class Jakartans shop at Pasaraya Grande – the city's largest and best-stocked department store; everyone else makes do with the colorful chaos of semi-outdoor shopping stalls, which offer terrific bargains and just about any fake branded item under the sun. The enormous Blok M bus terminal is one of the city's busiest, and a remarkable sight to behold. Frantic hawkers, blaring music, perplexed-looking passengers and overloaded buses darting in and out of crowded docks make this place a perfect microcosm of Jakarta itself.

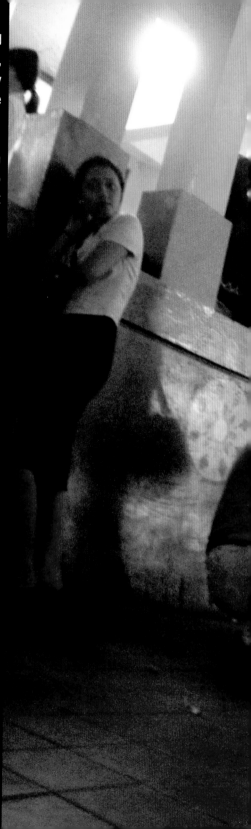

EVEN IN THESE post-colonial times, foreigners are an inseparable (and rather irritable) sub-species of Jakarta's human environment. As surely as Thailand has the *farang*, Singapore the *ang mo*, and Hong Kong the *gweilo*, so Jakarta has the *bule* (pronounced *"BOO-Leh"*) – its very own colloquial term for Westerners. The term comes from the word for 'albino' in Indonesian. Whether or not it is derogatory is a matter of interpretation: some foreigners resent the name, whilst others adopt it good-spiritedly and with a certain measure of self-irony. Most agree it is preferable to the other term incessantly hurled at foreigners in the street, the universal *"Miiisterrr!"*

An estimated 20,000 *bule* call Jakarta home (another 8,000 call Jakarta "a ghastly cloud of smog", but this statistic is unconfirmed). They are diplomats, journalists, consultants, bankers, artists, teachers, and NGO activists. They party hard, complain a fair bit, have many opinions, and holiday a lot. In fact, *bule* is not really a racial classification, but a mindset and wacky sub-culture all its own. Some *bule* are arrogant, bossy, or patronizing. Others are politically correct to the extreme, culturally oversensitive, or just totally neurotic. The spectacular theater that is a Jakarta expatriate's adaptation to local culture can resemble a poorly produced TV sit-com or a melodramatic Greek tragedy. Either way, it is a colorful process. There are of course character traits common to expatriates living anywhere in the world. But Jakarta's expats share a few particular, erm, 'behavioral responses' that set them apart. My friend Adrian Darmono, a leading Indonesian fashion designer and CBO (Certified *Bule* Observer), generously contributed his disturbing take on the subject (see box on following page).

27

YOU KNOW YOU'RE A BWM (Bule With A Mission) IF YOU …

- Embarrass Indonesian friends by dragging your driver into hip night clubs because you are such a NICE, DOWN-TO-EARTH kinda person…

- Cannot resist drawing parallels between shadow puppets, Javanese animist beliefs, and the political situation in Indonesia while boring dinner guests with pseudo-intellectual takes on current affairs

- Cannot simply buy friggin' souvenirs - instead, you are compelled to "make a contribution to the local economy…"

- Smugly mention you don't eat fried foods, with the exception of foods with exotic names like 'tofu', 'calamari', 'tempe', or 'tempura'. Fried Chicken? How pedestrian! How WESTERN!

- Own at least one book by celebrated Indonesian novelist Pramoedya Ananta Toer, and claim that you are "heavily into Indonesian literature…"

- Own at least one coffee table book with a title like *Contemporary Asian Tropical Interiors* or *Living with Batik*

- Act like you hate anything Western, and act "gee, shucks" apologetic for being one. Also apologize for colonialism, and for capitalism

- Listen to Paul Simon, Geoffrey Oryema, Nusrat Fateh Ali Khan, Gypsy Kings, or anything labeled 'world music'

- Make a demonstrative big deal out of liking chili sauce or durian fruit

- Work for a development agency or Non-Governmental Organization

- Rant about how Nike exploits its factory workers in Indonesia by paying them $35 a month

- Rave about how you can have breakfast in Indonesia for 10 cents

- Smile widely at everybody because you read somewhere that Indonesians are "by nature incredibly warm, friendly people"

- Think that Indonesian designers who don't use traditional fabrics are "ashamed of their heritage"

- Study obscure traditional Indonesian dance or musical instruments

- Have lots of rattan and/or teakwood furniture in your house

- Pretend you can't remember how to eat with a knife and fork

- Read books by Milan Kundera, Isabel Allende, Gabriel Garcia Marquez, or anything with political turmoil as a backdrop

- Watch movies (oops, FILMS!) by Roland Joffe, Chen Kaige, or anything with political turmoil as a backdrop

- Walk into a high-end boutique and say "What do you mean, I can't bargain here?! This is Indonesia!"

FAME IN INDONESIA is a strange creature, for few stars in Jakarta's entertainment scene are known solely as 'singers', 'actors' or 'models'. Rather, there is the generic, all-encompassing *artis*. The term refers to the city's great many celebrities who shamelessly cross artistic disciplines, starting out, say, in soap operas but moonlighting variously as talk show host, emcee, model and – if they can carry a tune – pop singer. These sorts of reincarnations are ostensibly the gift of multi-talented individuals, but are in fact often just cases of glamorous folks milking their name for all it's worth and spreading themselves way too thin in the process. The term *artis* is therefore a misnomer, for very little about what they do can be considered truly artistic.

But this doesn't mean they aren't revered by the public. On the contrary, celebrities bestowed with *artis* status need not do another film in their entire lives, nor cut a single decent album; they can safely retire to the salon and coffee shop circuit so long as they promise to feed the gossip mill every now and then by getting divorced, married, having an affair, or simply informing a local tabloid about their precious daughter's birthday bash or their trembling young son's circumcision party. Even if the *artis* hasn't produced a body of work in years, they'll still get invited to participate in TV talk shows, charity galas and gallery openings, so eternal is their standing in the public eye.

Jakarta is home to approximately 300 gossip and celebrity tabloids, whose admirable task is to keep abreast of all the important developments in the *artis* world. Indonesia's working class lives vicariously through these tabloids; drivers and housekeepers spend much of their free time watching soap operas on TV and soaking up the latest gossip about their favorite stars, so that the relationship becomes almost personal. In terms of pure entertainment value, the real-life soap opera of the *artis'* lives usually far out-dramatizes the televised version.

Lately, glitzy *artis* folk have infiltrated the world of fine arts as well. In an interesting, mutually beneficial trade-off, unlikely *artis* have been appearing on the theater or even poetry stage. This buys them considerable artistic prestige that they certainly don't gain in soap operas, while adding celebrity flare to otherwise dry, arty-farty events that would normally attract a crowd of around eleven dead-beat 'cultural activists'.

CELEBRITIES & 'ARTIS'

31

DEMO

A FEW YEARS BACK, a naughty political tabloid called *Tekad* published this curious series of photos. Three images shot at three separate and entirely unrelated political protests caught the very same demonstrator – a man dressed in each case in the very same clothing. He exemplified the peculiar *reformasi*-era trend of demonstrations as an industry, and demonstrators as nothing more than hired guns.

In these post-Soeharto years political demonstrations, known affectionately as *demo*, are an inseparable part of Jakarta's urban landscape. They hopelessly tie up traffic, but usually represent little more than petty power maneuvering amongst the country's political elite. If the Indonesian president, for instance, feels politically threatened, or the speaker of parliament is for some totally inexplicable reason being charged with corruption, these tortured souls

normally respond by arranging a series of *demo* to create the myth of public support. So most *demo* in Jakarta are not so much democratic expressions of public aspirations, but finely produced political theater serving dubious interests. To produce a *demo*, all you need is some money. (Luckily, presidents and speakers of parliament tend to have a bit of this.)

The *demo* industry is serious business. Certain impoverished, densely populated villages in Java are known as '*demo* villages'. Their residents - mostly manual laborers, farmers or unemployed youth – are happy to be recruited at a moment's notice for any *demo* in the capital, regardless of the stated message. Selecting a village is no random matter: some villages are known to be of a specific character and will be sourced for a certain type of demonstrator. Kampung Jaud, for instance, has earned a reputation as a rowdy, over-

populated village of criminals and hotheads, so its residents are perfect recruits for potentially unruly *demo* in the capital. Hired demonstrators receive anywhere from Rp 30-50,000 (around $3-5) per head for showing up, a boxed lunch and, for good measure, sometimes a pack of cigarettes. They are usually brought to the *demo* site in central Jakarta by chartered bus. For a quick-response *demo*, certain slums in the capital are known for their easy, immediate supply: at Kalipasir in Central Jakarta, for example, 100 demonstrators can usually be rounded up at a moment's notice.

These complex arrangements are always handled by a professional go-between whose job it is to receive an 'order' from the political interest group, recruit the necessary 'troops', and deliver a full-blown street production. He also serves as the 'guarantor', ensuring both that the hired crowd actually turns up, and that the 'client' pays up at the end of the day. In addition to this middleman, a *korlap* (*kordinator lapangan*, 'field coordinator') is on scene to handle transportation, the preparation and distribution of signs, banners and leaflets, and a timely provision of lunch to the edgy 'employees'. For his efforts, a *korlap* normally receives a fee of Rp 1.5-7 million (around $150-700), depending on experience and renown. He'll order *demo* paraphernalia, like banners, scarves and megaphones, usually through specialty suppliers in Jakarta's Senen Market.

With Jakarta *demo* so completely stage-managed, the intended ideological message often gets lost, or hilariously skewed. At one memorable *demo*, participants bussed in from Banten in West Java marched passionately under the slogan "Prepare to Launch Jihad to Resist Communist Students Who are Supported by Non-Islamic Blocks." Go figure.

33

DPR

THE SLOPING GREEN turtle-like roof of Indonesia's parliament building became a 'people power' icon to television viewers worldwide in May 1998, when a dramatic standoff between student democracy protesters and the government brought then-president Soeharto's 32-year dictatorship to an ungraceful end.

Tens of thousands of angry university students rallied for *reformasi* and occupied the compound of the People's Consultative Assembly. They demanded *Pak Harto*'s resignation and an end to the corrupt, oppressive New Order regime. But apparently that isn't all they did in the building's hallowed halls during those fateful few days in May. Journalists covering the story discovered used condoms in the hidden corners of MP cubicles, where students reportedly found time and energy for great sex in between heavy bouts of rallying under the hot sun in front of the world media. The revolution may have been televised, but the sexual revolution unfolded well out of camera view. After all, students of politics are taught that abstaining in parliament is a sign of indecisiveness. And who said young folks these days no longer give a f—k?

Moving right along.

DPR members are very special people, because they have agreed to sacrifice their own well-being to look after the well-being of all 210 million of Indonesia's citizens. Just to make sure they stay special, they get many special things. Like a big salary, huge health benefits, free trips overseas, and really nice cars. During official annual sessions, they get free room and board at the plush Mulia Senayan Hotel next door, ostensibly so that they don't have to battle traffic, which is usually caused by demonstrations the politicians themselves have organized and funded (see 'Demo' chapter).

For most Indonesians, the much-hyped myths of *reformasi* and *demokratisasi* have long been shattered. Political incompetence has destroyed much of their hope, and executive corruption still flourishes. But for a few glorious days back in May 1998, it seemed like 'people power' could make a lasting difference, and that the future just might be brighter. The Indonesian term for parliament, "People's Consultative Assembly" thus remains one of the greatest misnomers in this city.

DURIAN IS THE Southeast Asian 'King of Fruit' nobody can seem to ignore: in Singapore it is banned in public places due to its overpowering odor; in Bangkok its popularity is such that durian-flavored condoms are sold over the counter at any Seven Eleven. In Jakarta the fruit enjoys even greater prominence, and is sometimes thought to symbolize the city – large, spiky and smelly on the surface, soft and delicious inside. Hence Jakarta's nickname, the Big Durian.

Markets and supermarkets across Jakarta carry the unmistakable durian scent; ubiquitous branches of Dunkin Donuts are more likely to stock Durian Cream than Chocolate Glaze; and traditional cakes are cooked with a durian filling. Durian is the fruit Jakartans either love, or love to hate. Some take great pleasure in discussing its fine attributes, but others compare its taste to eating ice cream in a garbage dump. Durian is also thought to stimulate the libido. According to a Malay proverb, "when the durian falls down, the sarongs rise up."

Although the fruit is also grown in Thailand, the Philippines, and even Burma, it is native to Sumatra and Borneo, and the word *duri* means 'thorn' in Malay. Indonesia's finest durians are from North Sumatra, where the season lasts a full ten months. But Jakartans with money to burn opt for the much-revered and far pricier Mon Thong ('golden pillow') variety from Bangkok.

In Singaporean writer Hwee Hwee Tan's novel, *Mammon Inc.*, a durian vendor offers his own unique take on the fruit's many virtues:

> *"Durian, mister. Very nice. You see outside –" he pointed at the spikes on the fruit. "Sharp." He touched one of the spikes with his forefinger. "Ouch." He snickered. "You buy one, you got enemy, take durian, hit him on the head." He pretended to brain his assistant with the durian. "He sure die, ha, ha." He put the durian down on the table and took out a cleaver. "So you see, mister, durian, outside very dangerous, but inside…ahhhhh." He slammed down the cleaver and split the durian in half. He dug out the yellow, fleshy fruit from the shell. "Like gold nut. Soft gold."*

For true connoisseurs, selecting a durian is a ritual. They breathe in the scent, inspect the color, study the rind, and shake the fruit to check for loose seeds, which indicates ripeness. Some supermarkets offer precious samples from open durians to help customers decide. Durian is pried open with a large knife after locating a weak spot in the fruit's tough shell. Its rich yellowish pulp is then revealed, and eaten strictly with the fingers.

39

ES

BRIGHTLY COLORED *es* ('ice') beverages were a favorite street side Jakarta thirst-quencher long before all those sterile-looking 'pearl tea' drink stands took Asian and North American shopping malls by storm. *Es* drinks are very similar to their plastic-sealed brothers in the mall, but they're made with love, and cost one-tenth the price.

Foreign visitors are usually put off by the idea of digesting a very heavy dose of radiant, overly sweetened gelatin and fruit in Jakarta's midday heat. But for Jakartans, a big cool glass of *Es*-something is precisely the way to take the edge off a hot, stressful day, and just glimpsing a row of icy, rainbow-colored juice pitchers is already an energy-booster. They're affordable, too: A heaped serving of *es* costs Rp 1,000 to 2,000 (around 10 to 20 cents), depending on the type of beverage. *Es* is more snack than beverage and usually so packed with fruit and various other particles that it is eaten with a spoon rather than just sipped with a straw.

The popular *Es Cendol* mixes jackfruit, palm sugar, coconut milk and green gelatin-like particles made from mung bean flour, and topped with a generous dose of crushed ice that absorbs the drink's flavor and color. There are many variants on this drink, such as the addition of boiled kidney beans.

The milky-white *Es Kelapa Muda* ('young coconut juice') combines ice-cold sweet coconut milk with coconut shavings; *Es Alpukat* is a sweetened avocado juice diluted with water, often with chocolate mixed in; *Es Buah* or *Es Campur* include an assorted mixture of fruits, condensed milk, syrup and crushed ice; *Es Juice* is a crushed ice version of various tropical fruit juices.

GAMBIR

PEOPLE ALWAYS COMPLAIN about Gambir, but Jakarta's busiest train station is a great travel hub for destinations throughout Java, and happens to be a truly quirky place. For starters, hundreds of over-eager, luggage-hauling 'coolies' zip around the station in numbered orange jerseys like underpaid football players on steroids. Next, the whole place is done up in a puke-green hue, so that it looks like a semi-outdoor hospital with very high ceilings. The vomit theme continues with most of the donuts sold at the refreshment stalls: you wouldn't want to be stuck on a thirteen-hour train ride after eating a few of those. On the subject of donuts, Gambir is a classic place to witness one of Indonesia's most time-honored traditions: the 'Bring-the-Relatives-Some-Dunkin'-Donuts-as-a-Souvenir-From-the-Big-City' ritual. This curious custom made sense back when Jakarta had the only Dunkin' Donuts in the archipelago: folks would impress country-bum relatives by arriving with a shiny box of Western delights from the ultramodern capital. These days, bright pink Dunkin' Donuts branches are found in any small town in Indonesia, particularly at provincial train stations. So the big question is, why in this day and age do people still insist on showing up with Dunkin' gift boxes when their relatives can buy the stuff at the very same station where they're being met? Nobody knows for sure.

Next mystery. Who are the smiling little guys in flip-flops who whisper and shuffle between rows of passengers queuing at Gambir ticket booths? These are of course scalpers, or *calo*. Whenever seats on a train are sold out, these upstanding young men miraculously show up to offer passengers the very tickets they sought – at a significantly inflated price. And the reason tickets are so frequently sold out is that the same scalpers buy them all up in advance. Often, as many as 100 scalpers stand in line to buy tickets for a single train. Some *calo* even receive phone-in orders from regular customers via Gambir's official information booth phone! It's a neat little system. The fasting month of Ramadan is peak season for *calo*: the station feels like a refugee camp as thousands of wannabe passengers park themselves for hours in front of the ticket booths in the hopes of securing a seat for *pulang kampung* ('returning to the village'). As customers grow increasingly desperate, *calo* demand double or even triple the official price. Attempts to rid Gambir of *calo* have been half-hearted; station ticket sale officers are in on ticket deals, so nobody wants to rock the boat.

42

INDONESIA MAY BE a predominantly Muslim country, but Jakarta's gay community enjoys a remarkable degree of openness and freedom. In part, this is because the government position on homosexuality is that it doesn't exist. The issue is therefore not addressed, and there are no formal restrictions within the law. So while homosexuality is generally shunned within traditional Muslim and Christian families in Indonesia, Jakarta's social scene is an entirely different matter.

Not to be confused with the city's sidelined *waria* ('lady boy') class, members of Jakarta's mainstream gay community socialize at ultra-trendy parties and clubs. Gay icons here are frequently embraced by the media as messengers of new fads and cutting-edge fashion. As in other cosmopolitan cities around the world, a great number of Jakarta's top designers, artists, media executives, hairdressers, socialites, TV hosts and actors are openly gay. Their influence even extends to colloquial banter, and Jakarta street slang can be traced in part to gay jargon. *Bahasa Gaul* – the crass *lingua franca* of the city's teenage mall rats – for instance, borrows many words from the contemporary gay vocabulary. Everyday terms for gays include *g* and *binan,* and the more derogatory *hombreng, sekong* and *sakinah*. But the most common is simply *gay*.

Jakarta's 'cruising' scene is pretty full on. Glitzy shopping malls are the prime hunting ground for young gay men, particularly Plaza Indonesia in central Jakarta. In the city's Senen district, a certain mainstream cinema has earned renown as a unique gay cruising spot: when the lights go out and the film begins, members of the audience begin to mingle anonymously…

In recent years a handful of up-market clubs have introduced gay nights. The most popular venue even stages an elaborate cabaret show with dozens of performers gloriously done up in drag. And a gay film retrospective organized by the innovative TUK cultural center (see 'TUK & TIM' chapter) drew larger crowds than any of their previous cinematic programs, and no protest whatsoever. But more than anything else, discreet gay chat rooms on the internet are mushrooming at a staggering rate, and have quickly become the Jakarta gay community's most lively meeting place. Perhaps a sign that despite all the open partying, gay lifestyle isn't yet as publicly accepted as it seems.

UNDER a New Order regime obsessed with the 'communist threat', public expressions of Chinese culture were banned for years in Indonesia. When that regime was toppled in 1998 and the economy lay in shambles, Chinese-Indonesians paid the price as rioters swept through their North Jakarta neighborhoods, looted shops, burned buildings and raped women. Thousands of ethnic Chinese fled to Hong Kong or Singapore. The cultural ban wasn't lifted until 2000. The rape cases still haven't been properly investigated, much less brought to trial. But Jakarta's Chinese community is gradually getting back on its feet, and its 'Chinatown', Glodok, is back in business.

Business is key here. From traditional market stalls to huge electronic mega-malls, everyone seems to be trading something. The outdoor market along Jalan Pancoran carries snakes, frogs, turtles, herbal medicine, exotic fruits, home hardware, firecrackers, pornographic VCDs, traditional Chinese cakes, and of course a breast-enlarging potion made from tarantula extract.

The alleyways here are home to some of the best noodle stalls in Jakarta, and a narrow lane, Petak Sembilan, leads through a charming wet market straight to the courtyard of Jakarta's most ornate Confucian temples, or *klenteng*. Inside, worshipers busily shuffle from one altar to the next, lighting incense and uttering prayers. The energy is remarkable, as are the soft rays of light that slip through the ceiling beams, and the two-meter-tall candles that burn for six months and weigh up to 300kg. Try putting one of those on a little girl's birthday cake.

Chinese culture is practiced openly once again; Jakarta now has a number of Mandarin-language daily newspapers, and Chinese New Year celebrations are felt throughout the city. At night, it gets wilder still (see 'Kota Nightlife' chapter), as enormous dance clubs, karaoke lounges and casinos take charge of the scene, and street side dining stalls serve up piping hot portions of monkey meat.

49

WHEN PEOPLE THINK of the Golden Triangle, it's usually the wild, rugged meeting point of Thailand, Burma and Laos. Images of vast green poppy fields, opium trade and general lawlessness spring to mind. Jakarta's version of the Golden Triangle is only slightly different. While there isn't much of an opium trade here, and certainly no poppy fields, lawlessness is everywhere, for this district is home to most of Jakarta's domestic and international banks. And since Indonesia is consistently ranked one of the most corrupt countries on earth, these banks tend to resemble laundromats more than prudent financial institutions.

The 'triangle' is demarcated by the city's main boulevards – Jalan Sudirman, Jalan Gatot Subroto and Jalan Rasuna Said. Jakarta's prime apartment space is located here, as are a majority of the city's 5-star hotels. From a distance, the Golden Triangle's towering skyscrapers – some crowned with their own helipads – lend Jakarta the appearance of a prospering metropolis.

Closer inspection, however, reveals hundreds of low-rent *kampung* (see 'Slums' chapter) crammed between the massive structures of glass, concrete and steel. Often they are literally just structures, as Indonesia's monetary crisis (see 'Krismon' chapter) halted virtually all of the city's construction activity in the late 1990s. Half-finished projects and empty lots are a common sight off these main roads, although lately, building efforts have resumed.

But financial ruin hasn't killed the human buzz of Jakarta's fastest-moving quarter. Theme cafes, wine bars, pubs and ethnic restaurants are tucked into its many office buildings, giving Jakarta yuppies a wide choice of places for power lunches or chilling out at the end of a long work day. State-of-the-art fitness clubs give office folks a place to work off the stress, while the district's many shopping centers, boutiques and salons give them ample opportunity to blow all their money – if and when the economy picks up again.

GOLDEN TRIANGLE

53

GOLF

MANY OF JAKARTA'S beautifully trimmed golf courses boast a unique, added virtue: they double as historical sites. This is because they were built on land previously occupied by slums and rural villages, and nobody knows the precise fate of the unfortunate farmers and residents who were forced to make room for the playgrounds of Jakarta's crony class. We do know that some of the country's largest conglomerates moved swiftly and mercilessly to clear land for what in the 1980s was fast becoming Asia's favorite new hobby. Bulldozers literally rolled across vegetable plantations and farmers were ordered to re-settle elsewhere with little or no compensation. That hasn't stopped anyone from teeing off, though, and rather sadly the whopping 38 golf courses across Greater Jakarta represent the closest thing the city has to public parks.

Golf courses are where Jakarta cronies and politicians conduct business. But they attract many happy foreign visitors too, because by international golf standards they offer great value: Most of Jakarta's courses are world class, and some charge as little as Rp 110,000 (about $11) per round on a weekday. Not surprisingly, caddies come cheap and plentiful too, so that even the most hopeless golfer can enjoy the delusion of being Tiger Woods – in between swings, anyway.

GORENGAN

EVERYTHING IS RELATIVE. American-style fast food might be bad for you, but Jakarta's deep-fried street-side snacks known as *gorengan* make KFC or McDonald's seem like farm-grown organic health food by comparison.

Gorengan literally means 'fried things', a fitting term considering that the tofu, bananas, and vegetable cakes are mercilessly soaked in boiling oil until thoroughly dripping. Yeah, they taste good. And they're cheap. And they are found at stalls on virtually every street corner in the city, or sold in neatly wrapped plastic bags at traffic junctions or along busy toll roads. Which explains why *gorengan* remain one of the city's most popular snacks amongst late night office workers, hungry students and cash-strapped slum dwellers.

A typical *gorengan* stall will offer any number of fried delights, usually *tahu* (tofu), *tempe* (bean curd), *pisang* (bananas), *risol* (vermicelli spring rolls), *sagu* (sago), *singkong* (cassava), *ubi* (sweet potato) and *bakwan* (veggie cakes). A portion of street side *gorengan* typically costs around Rp 300 (3 cents). A somewhat up-market variation on the *gorengan* theme has in recent years emerged in the form of fried chicken stalls that sell a greasy breast or thigh for as little as Rp 1,500 (15 cents) – dangerous competition for KFC and its kind. In fact, some of these stalls even advertise themselves as...'Kentaki Fraid Chiken'. They'd better be prepared for a possible traidmarck lawsoot.

HANDPHONES

AN IMAGE THAT LINGERED after my first stay in Jakarta in 1991 was of people patiently lining up outside *wartel* phone offices to use a metered payphone (see 'Wartel & Warnet' chapter). Today the image would be of people colliding head-on in shopping malls because their eyes are glued to their mobile phone screens as they frantically punch short text messages into the keypad.

But forget 'mobile' or 'cell' phone. In Jakarta, those radiation-emitting things we bark loudly into in the middle of a cinema or a classy restaurant are known as handphones, or simply HP ("Hah-Peh"). And handphones in Jakarta are tantamount to identity. If you don't have one, you don't really exist.

The obsession with handphones is surprising considering the current tattered state of the Indonesian economy. But these days handphones far outnumber land lines in Jakarta, and people here seem hell bent on communicating anywhere and anytime, no matter the cost. Nor are handphones restricted to the city's elite: taxi drivers, bar girls, fish market vendors and even bus musicians can be seen carrying them.

A few things about Jakarta give handphones added currency. For starters, getting stuck in one of the city's notorious traffic jams (see 'Macet' chapter) make having a HP quite essential when you're running late for a crucial meeting. And in a tumultuous climate of riots and political demonstrations, protesters and activists use them regularly to network and to mobilize demonstrators.

Short Message Service (SMS) texting is a fast, cheap way of communicating utter nonsense, and so has lately become an obsession amongst Jakarta's teenagers and mall rats. Also popular these days is that plague on modern society called the downloadable ring tone. The sound of a ghastly electronic version of the latest Celine Dion ballad coming from a neighboring table at a café is sufficient to ruin one's day.

Ownership of a cutting-edge model, particularly by Nokia, has also become something of fashion statement. After the requisite heavy promotional campaign, one will be persuaded to go out and buy it. That is, one and about 999,999 other sheep. Hence the term *HP sejuta umat,* or 'HP of a million people'. The desire to be a bit different has led to the mushrooming in Jakarta malls of tiny stalls that are effectively handphone service stations. Here, handsets can be customized to the heart's fulfillment. Flashing antennas, Hello Kitty keypads, interchangeable faces…you name it, they've got it.

A popular stunt amongst Jakarta's cash-strapped teenagers is the 'missed call' phenomenon. While these youngsters would sell their grandmother for a handset, they can't always afford the pre-paid credit vouchers to place calls. So a credit-less teen will dial a friend, let it ring on the other end, and hang up, hoping the other party will know who called, and ring them back. Unless the friend, too, is out of credits. An alternative to this game: some cellular providers don't charge for the first three seconds of a call. Frugal teenagers exploit this by making repeat three-second calls, cramming in as much as they can say in the duration.

HOTEL INDONESIA

AT FIRST GLANCE the dilapidated hotel on Jakarta's busiest traffic circle looks quite unexceptional, but it's actually a curious landmark. Known locally by its acronym, HI (pronounced "Hah-Eee"), the hotel is an eerie symbol of President Sukarno's obsessive 1960s effort to create a 'New Jakarta' that would bring international respect to his nation and pride to his struggling people. Opened with great hoopla in 1962, Hotel Indonesia epitomized the era's modernization drive, and in a retro sort of way has become the stuff of legends. The lobby still displays evidence from that golden period: a photo of their very first guest, a visibly perspiring American named Allen Alwelt, who worked for the Rockefeller Foundation and is seen arriving in a *becak* and wearing what the caption describes as "an ordinary shirt with no jacket, and brown cotton trousers"; a 1972 photo of a Bee Gees appearance at the hotel's Nirwana Supper Club; a snapshot of a visit by Senator Robert Kennedy.

Australian journalist Christopher Koch described it thus in his colorful novel-turned-Hollywood film, *The Year of Living Dangerously,* set in 1965:

> The fourteen-story Hotel Indonesia (always with a capital H) rode like a luxury ship in mid-ocean, being at this time the only one of its kind in the whole country. It stood in New Jakarta; and like Friendship Square, and Jalan Thamrin – the six-lane highway that carried the traffic here from the Old City – it had recently been ordered into being by President Sukarno, who considered an international hotel necessary to the nation's prestige. Paid for by the Japanese, managed by the Americans, it had its own power supply (since Jakarta's was fast failing); its own purified water (since Jakarta's now carried infections); its own frigid air, which no other hotel could offer. Food was flown in from San Francisco and Sydney, or grown on the hotel's own farm. With its restaurants, night-clubs, bars, swimming pool, and shops, it was a world complete. It was also majestically expensive; but heat or gastritis usually broke the resolve of those transients who tried the decaying colonial hotels of the Old City.

These days, 'decaying' best describes Hotel Indonesia itself – reduced through neglect to a sad echo of its former glory and overtaken literally on all sides by gleaming new international-chain hotels. No longer a home-away-from-home for glamorous foreign dignitaries and celebrities, today the hotel mainly hosts tired Indonesian civil servants and political party hacks attending seminars in the capital. Guests are only half-jokingly advised by friends in the know to arrive with their own supply of *Baygon* mosquito repellant. Art exhibits in the main atrium showcase some of the tackiest Indonesian paintings imaginable (think images of horses galloping into the sunset, made from feathers; think Balinese dancers against a backdrop of snow-capped mountains). And five red-and-white ceramic Indonesian flags still loom large over the lobby, greeting visitors at what often feels like a theme park of Indonesian nationalism.

KE SO MANY backpackers on Lonely Planetized journeys through Southeast Asia, was introduced to Jakarta through the seedy traveler haunt of Jalan Jaksa – a 500-meter stretch of hot dusty pavement in the heart of the city. It's not a pretty place.

Decades ago, weary travelers en route from Sumatra to Sulawesi stopped here to rest over coffee and banana jaffles, and plan the next leg of their Great Archipelago Adventure. Some buried their sunburned faces in crusty second-hand books and searched for their inner selves. Jalan Jaksa was a quiet street then, with a few cheap hostels and little else.

Enter a blaring re-mix of Eminem's latest single and the set changes dramatically. Small open-air bars now fill the gaps between hostels, and the atmosphere is decidedly more sinister. Nobody seems to notice the second-hand book stalls anymore; and Muslim fundamentalist groups have lately made a habit of conducting 'moral sweeps' along the street, breaking down bar doors and smashing bottles of alcohol. With cheap beer and even cheaper women, Jalan Jaksa has firmly established itself as a down-market hub of sinful pleasures.

Nigerian drug-dealers in silk shirts and gold rings linger in fluorescent-lit drinking dens. A new generation of backpackers and surfer dudes hangs out at bars called Memories and BFC; these days they seem not so much into finding themselves as losing themselves in the sickly delights of watered down cocktails with names like 'Slippery Nipple'. Male travelers are sometimes flanked by heavily perfumed, platform wearing local honeys. The boys' smug young faces suggest they don't realize they'll have to pay these 'friendly ladies' for their services later on, or that some of these friendly ladies aren't ladies at all.

Alongside the travelers, middle-aged hippies look as though they've been here twenty years too long and gone a bit mad in the process. Many are Jaksa veterans from the 1970s who apparently forgot to ever go home; they continue living and teaching English in Jakarta, and warm their favorite Jaksa bar stools practically every night of the week. Late opening hours, cheap beer and the informal atmosphere have lured even ordinary young Indonesians to the street in recent years: student activists, young screenwriters and intellectuals have adopted Jaksa as a favorite venue for meetings into the night.

During the peak traveler season of June through August, the bars and hostels fill with jaded but happily boozed-up kids, prostitutes and Top 40 hits. Just as in the 1970s, local children gaze in from the perimeter in utter amazement, waiting for another fight to erupt between Swedish or German boyband lookalikes. The children's expressions haven't changed. Only the young, white people on the other side of the perimeter have.

JAMU

IF ONE THING in Jakarta's modern urban mess still evokes images of a tranquil Javanese village, it is the door-to-door sellers of *jamu* – Indonesian traditional herbal medicine. These *jamu gendong* ladies carry on their backs baskets stacked with colorful bottled remedies. Walk down any Jakarta side street in the early morning or late afternoon, and you could be in a back alley of Yogyakarta, Semarang or Solo.

This all sounds very serene, but here's the dirty truth behind all the beautiful mystical talk: *jamu* is first and foremost about increasing sexual drive. Yep, jamu is to Indonesians what *mojo* is to Austin Powers. And just as our favorite International Man of Mystery wouldn't go a day without *mojo*, many Jakartans drink a healthy portion of bottled, murky-colored liquid before leaving for work each morning. Or just check out all the men who congregate at roadside '*jamu* bars' to down a glass or two of powder-mixed *Kuku Bima*, a popular aphrodisiac.

But *jamu* is much more than just traditional Viagra. A staggering range of drinks, powders, capsules, and pills are thought to cure practically every disease known to man – and woman. Indeed, women are particularly fond of jamu as a remedy for everything from menstrual pain and oily skin to swollen feet and fertility problems. There are even formulas for 'producing a tight vagina' or 'ensuring a harmonious marriage'.

Around 900 various plant, tree, fruit, and oil extracts are used in making *jamu*. Candlenut, galangal, *kencur* (resurrection lily), turmeric and nutmeg are some of the most common. *Jamu* in its various forms can be bought in supermarkets, kiosks, specialty boutiques and fresh markets. There are now around 500 industrial-scale *jamu* manufacturers in Indonesia. It's a huge market: an estimated 5 million doses of the stuff are consumed here daily. But the door-to-door *jamu gendong* sellers usually prepare their liquids at home. Their basket of bottles – slung by an old strip of batik cloth – can weigh as much as 20kg. Traditionally, a basket containing an even number of bottles means the seller is married; an odd number suggests she is still single.

Despite its traditional qualities, *jamu* plays a major role in contemporary life in Jakarta. Everyone from slum-dwellers to yuppies and government ministers seems to be hooked on some form of herbal cure. Even those with access to the latest innovations in Western medicine will often chug a dose or two of jamu, "just in case…"

KARAOKE

THE WORD, we're reminded in so many pop culture essays in the Asia edition of *Time* magazine, is Japanese for 'empty orchestra'. In Indonesian it might as well translate as 'plush, overcrowded room full of drunk yuppies vying for the microphone and howling offensive boyband tunes'. True Jakarta karaoke fiends know how to choose the kind of sappy numbers that would make most normal people physically ill. But the die-hards croon like they mean it, and karaoke in Jakarta is more about the uninhibited social atmosphere than the vomit-inducing music. Karaoke is popular for birthday outings, business get-togethers, or whenever there appears to be nothing more exciting going on in town on a Saturday night. Incredibly, some karaoke lounges in Jakarta are open 24 hours, so if you're overcome by a sudden urge to belt out 'Hey Jude' after your morning *bubur ayam* porridge, do not despair. The genre is so popular that many Executive Class trains from Jakarta to Central Java are now equipped with 'karaoke cars', where passengers can sing the night away while heading for Solo (and perhaps a solo career).

Serious karaoke lounges are typically divided into private 'living rooms' of various sizes, rented by the hour. Naughty lounges include an attached bedroom (for those who can't sing but whose talents presumably lie elsewhere). Normally there's a three-hour minimum, but it's amazing how time flies when you're belting out heart-on-the-sleeve renditions of 'Careless Whisper' and 'I Will Survive'. Shoes come off, sofas are leapt upon, and menus strewn around the room offer beer and food and a huge selection of songs in English, Indonesian and Mandarin. Patrons select videos via microphone from operators, who in a frantic control room jump over each other to feed the many laser disc machines and keep up with requests. Newer venues in Jakarta have started using automated computers that spin DVDs. For the uninitiated, karaoke videos are – without even meaning to be – hilarious spectacles most often depicting a bored-looking couple strolling awkwardly hand in hand along a beach in South Java. The climax is when they locate a shimmering rock, sit down on it and ponder the waves. Then the man hands a red rose to his adoring companion. Racy stuff. Song lyrics scroll across the bottom of the screen, sometimes with horrendous errors in transliteration.

KEMANG

FUNNY HOW SO MANY foreigners posted to Indonesia (see 'Bule' chapter) receive 'hardship' or 'danger' allowances. Judging from the cushy lifestyle in the expatriate enclave of Kemang in South Jakarta, hardship doesn't seem at all relevant to the equation (except to the extent that it's hard to get up for work after a hard night of hard drinking and partying).

Kemang is Jakarta's quintessential expatriate bubble. Though not quite a gated community, it's a self-contained neighborhood with everything from up-market boutiques and concept dining to exclusive international schools, chic bookshops, luxury spas, trendy noodle bars and even a bona fide Salsa club. Specialty supermarket Kemchiks is considered so central to the expat experience that ads in *The Jakarta Post* for Kemang homes often specify the property's distance from this hallowed bastion of imported goods. To demarcate the neighborhood, an enormous traffic jam runs all the way around its perimeter at nearly all hours of the day. Here's to one way streets!

Some people (never me, of course) like to sneer at this sort of head-in-the-sand existence, but to be fair, Kemang is more than just an overpriced cultural incubator. The neighborhood is also home to some very pleasant garden cafes, huge grassy back yards and wonderful art and photo galleries – rare delights in a city dominated by concrete, asphalt and shopping malls. And each year the Kemang Fair is the closest thing Jakarta has to a neighborhood street bazaar.

UNIVERSITY STUDENTS and young professionals in Jakarta generally either live at home with their parents or 'alone', which probably means they live in a *kos* – rows of simple rooms that are Indonesia's version of students halls of residence or dormitories.

The term *kos* (or sometimes *kost*) comes from the Dutch term *in de kost*, meaning boarding in a family home and paying on a monthly basis. Indeed, this form of living arrangement dates far back into the Dutch colonial era, and even writings on founding Indonesian president Soekarno frequently mention how he lived "*indekos*" while a student at university in Bandung in the 1920s.

Perhaps one reason it can take as long as ten years to complete an undergraduate degree in Indonesia is the students' hopeless addiction to laid-back *kos-kosan* life. Besides a rather spartan room and dubious kitchen and bathroom facilities, the *kos* setup usually offers proximity to the city center, freedom from parents and household responsibilities, and a built-in social scene complete with gossip, scandal and endless personal drama. In short, it is Melrose Place on a budget, minus the swimming pool. Countless hours – no, entire years – are wasted away on the corridor floor adjoining the *kos* rooms; activities range from impromptu guitar singalongs to chess and card playing, political activism and late night heart-to-heart exchanges. Many graduates don't abandon the *kos* lifestyle at all: upon completing their degree, they take a job in the city and move into yet another *kos* – an upscale version inhabited by young professionals.

The cost of renting a room in a *kos* depends on facilities and location. A simple student *kos* way out in Depok near the University of Indonesia campus can be had for around Rp 100,000 (around $10) per month and includes a tiny room with a bed, desk and cupboard, communal bathrooms and free laundry service. By contrast, yuppies working in the heart of Jakarta's central business district will spend as much as Rp 900,000 (around $90) per month on a luxury *kos*, meaning a 'studio'-style room just minutes away from the office, with air-con, cable TV, cleaning service and private bathroom with hot water shower.

In the past, *kos* lifestyle was marked by the looming (and usually plump) figure of an *Ibu Kos* ("*Kos* Mother") – an omnipresent maternal authority who lived on site and would intervene in domestic matters, enforce curfews, keep members of the opposite sex from hanging around too long, and generally ensure residents didn't step out of line. These days, *kos* offer more privacy and sometimes even co-ed living. They are often set up by wealthy families as a side business, and managed remotely with the help of a friendly maid or maintenance man.

KOTA NIGHTLIFE

WHEN PEOPLE CLAIM Jakarta's nightlife is one of the best-kept secrets in Asia, they are probably referring to the clubbing and entertainment scene of the city's northern quarter known as Kota. By day it masquerades as Chinatown's bustling commercial district. When night falls, the place transforms into a wild nocturnal playground, and little of what goes on there is legal.

Monster clubs like Stadium, Millennium, Sydney 2000, Raja Mas and 1001 are one-stop dens of unbridled pleasure. Stadium is so thumping these days that on weekends – from Thursday evening until Monday morning – it never shuts. The busiest time on its psychedelic dance floor is Sunday at about 9AM, when clubbers are 'coming down' from an all-night 'trip'.

A typical Kota club is split into a few floors, each offering a different 'activity'. Ravers take in heaving techno beats in a cavernous, pitch-dark central dance hall. This is also where drugs – mostly ecstasy pills – are consumed en mass. The club management doesn't deal drugs directly, but allows an external dealer to operate within the venue, so that someone is accountable if things go wrong. Management will receive at least Rp 150 million (around $15,000) per month just for 'leasing' its turf to the dealer. To further shield the club from official involvement in drugs, ecstasy is mostly sold in the back parking lot, where a pill trades for about Rp 50,000-100,000 (around $5 to $10).

Pills purchased inside – where waiters act as 'runners' - can cost four times as much, as the risk of a police raid is higher there. Besides the main dance floor, clubs usually house a karaoke level with private singing rooms, where male clientele are accompanied by hostesses who double as strippers; a live music floor, where a 'mama-san' introduces glassy-eyed guests to giggly bar girls; and the natural extension of all that – a 'love hotel' floor, where guests and their bar girls can get better acquainted.

The real money in Kota isn't from bar girls, or karaoke, or even ecstasy. Gambling is the biggest game in town, operating both within these clubs and at separate, much larger gambling dens nearby. Revenues must be enormous, because clubs fork out Rp 800 million to Rp 1.5 billion (around $80,000 to $150,000) each month in protection money for their gambling operations. Jakarta even has its very own 'Godfather' of gambling who calls all the shots and is so powerful that he's known as 'K1', a code meaning Chief of Police. There's talk of shifting the city's gambling operations to offshore casinos on Pulau Seribu, or 'Thousand Islands', presumably modeled on Malaysia's Genting Highlands. But for the time being Kota is still alive with the sound of poker machines, roulette and blackjack tables. And smaller activities like slot machines and Togel, a numbers game insanely popular amongst working class men, will likely remain a Kota fixture for quite some time.

KRATING DAENG

ENERGY DRINKS are probably not the healthiest thing on earth. But if you've ever had to watch your taxi driver nod off to sleep with the car doing 130kph down one of Jakarta's main thoroughfares at night, you might recognize a redeeming quality in those punchy little bottles.

Red Bull's official website plugs its controversial syrupy-sweet brew as the drink "for when a long day is over and a long night starts," and for "long, sleep inducing motorways." No wonder its Thai originator, *Krating Daeng*, is the beverage of choice for so many of Jakarta's groggy-eyed cabbies. Sometimes dubbed "the poor man's coffee" of Asia, *Krating Daeng* (Thai for 'red bull') took off in Bangkok in the early eighties. In recent years the drink has shifted upmarket to win over Asian yuppies, from 'E'-popping clubbers to workaholic dot-commers. But its real customer base remains the many long-haul truckers and taxi drivers struggling through 20-hour shifts. Many Jakarta cabbies admit to being addicted to the drink, and down four or five bottles of it a day.

Nasty rumors have dogged the manufacturer for years: That the stuff's made from bull semen; that it's an ecstasy-type stimulant; that it contains amphetamine. In reality, *Krating Daeng* is a very potent mix of taurin (an amino acid that kick-starts the metabolism), caffeine, sugar and vitamin Bs. Competing Asian 'health tonics' – Lipovitan, M-150 or Extra Joss for instance – contain similar mixtures. Energy drinks offer a sensation that in some ways reflects Jakarta itself: a wonderful 'high' marked by a real buzz, only to fade quickly, leaving you feeling pretty drained.

KRETEK

JAKARTA SHARES MANY of its aromas – like those from rotting sewage and thick black traffic fumes – with many big capitals in the developing world. But like these other cities, Jakarta possesses trademark aromas all its own, such as those from roadside *nasi goreng*, durian fruit and of course the unmistakable, sweet scent of *kretek* clove cigarettes.

Kretek smoking is arguably Indonesia's national pastime – born and bred on the island of Java nearly a century ago. *Kretek* contain tobacco just like in regular cigarettes but in typical Indonesian fashion, a whole variety of spices and flavors are thrown in for good measure. All *kretek* contain cloves, plus as many as a hundred other subtle flavors like rum and pineapple.

While there are over 500 *kretek* producers in Indonesia today, Jakarta is the playground for big boys like Sampoerna, Djarum and Gudang Garam – as is plainly apparent from their aggressive advertising in and around the city. Advertisements range from massive 20-meter illuminated billboards to posters slapped on bridges and underpasses. Ads are sometimes even painted across buses that dart around the city. *Kretek* companies love the whole 'cultural sponsorship' thing, too. At just about any rock concert in Jakarta, catching a new, kick-ass band nearly always involves free samples of a new, kick-ass brand.

Jakartans smoke practically everywhere – in taxis, elevators, government offices, petrol stations and hospital maternity wards. The only odd exceptions seem to be McDonalds (unless you hide in the corner) and the airport (although the burnt waste bins suggest enforcement hasn't been too rigorous).

A curious feature of Jakarta – indeed, of the entire archipelago – is the total absence of cigarette vending machines. One possible reason for this: in local currency a few dozen coins would be necessary to add up to the required amount, and most banknotes here are so ratty they would never be recognized by an electronic device. The main reason is that *kretek* are stocked behind the counter of nearly any eating or drinking establishment in the city. On the off chance that they are not, one of the service staff will gladly run out to the street to grab a pack of your favorite brand (cash up front, of course).

KRISMON

CONSIDER THIS BLURB A TRIBUTE. To an awful economic mess that began in this region in 1997, shook global money markets, and left the Indonesian economy in tatters. The story of *krismon* (short for *krisis moneter*, or 'monetary crisis') hardly makes headlines anymore, but for most Indonesians it hasn't gone away at all. To discuss contemporary Jakarta without mentioning *krismon* would be doing an injustice to millions whose lives have been turned upside down by rampant corruption, a collapsed banking system, and the dangerous myth that was the Asian Economic Miracle.

Krismon means different things to different Jakartans. Many lost their jobs; some went from eating meat with their rice most nights of the week, to never eating it at all; others could no longer afford even cooking oil after basic subsidies were suddenly removed. A former banker began selling sandwiches to office workers. Newly unemployed celebrities earned a living opening charming roadside cafés that served cash-strapped yuppies who could no longer dine at swanky restaurants. People from all walks of life were affected, but somehow, most managed to get by.

Things are a bit better now. GDP is on the rise, the badly damaged Rupiah regained some of its value, and unemployment figures are somewhat better than they were a few years back. But Jakarta has been traumatized by the crisis. Concrete skeletons of unfinished skyscrapers are eerie monuments to the *krismon* experience. The city's many luxury cars reflect not just excessive wealth in the hands of a dubious few, but also attempts by their owners to protect funny money from the debt collector's reach.

Each year in Jakarta we optimistically repeat the same stupid joke: that this coming December *krismon* will finally be over because it becomes 'krismas'...

Christmas still hasn't arrived.

LATE NIGHT SNACKS, or *jajanan malam*, is the Jakarta equivalent of England's post-clubbing doner kebab or America's 24-hour fast food drive-thru. It is the fuel of urban night owls, a nocturnal ritual that not only eases hunger pangs but is an inseparable part of any serious night on the town. The typically rustic, dimly lit setting is also a popular choice of venue for a first date – far less intimidating than a fancy restaurant and certainly a whole lot cheaper. Seating is on narrow benches or plastic stools, although many folks prefer drive-up style, and are served through the window of their car.

You can find nearly every kind of Indonesian cuisine on the street at night, from chicken sate to fried noodles, *ketoprak* and *siomay*, but the following no-nonsense delicacies typify the Jakarta late night street dining experience:

Bubur Ayam is a rice-based porridge made with shredded chicken, deep-fried soybeans, chives, sweet soy sauce and chili. It's popular both late at night and as an early-morning breakfast, and is similar to Chinese congee, but with a far thicker consistency. There are numerous street porridge variations – like the veggie-based *Bubur Manado* and green bean *Bubur Kacang* – but a heaping bowl of classic chicken *bubur* is what really makes Jakartans salivate.

Roti Bakar is essentially grilled bread, but with a hundred different variations depending on the filling. Savory fillings include cheese, thinly sliced sausage, and fried egg. Sweet fillings include *kaya* – a cloudy spread made from coconut milk, sugar and eggs – as well as chocolate spread, peanut butter, and strawberry jam. This stuff is super cheap and considered classic post-clubbing fare.

Nasi Goreng, or fried rice, is arguably Indonesia's most famous dish. Although dumbed-down versions now adorn the menus of chic ethnic restaurants everywhere from Melbourne to San Francisco, Jakartans truly cannot seem to get enough of this original roadside grub, and devour platefuls of the stuff with great urgency and animated delight. At Rp 3,000 (around 30 cents) per hearty plate, it's one of the best value dinners money can buy.

Martabak comes in two completely different forms: *manis* (sweet) and *telor* (egg-based, or savory). *Manis* is thought to originate from Bangka island, and is best described as a thick, flying-saucer-shaped waffle stuffed with chocolate sprinkles, peanuts and cheese. We're talking five-digit calorie counts per portion here, but hey, some things are best ignored. *Martabak Telor* has its roots in India, and is a flat, square, deep-fried pancake stuffed with minced beef, eggs and shredded vegetables. It doesn't boast as many calories as sweet *martabak*, but it swims in so much oil for so long that nobody will mistake it for health food.

THE TERM HAS a sleazy ring to it, and to be sure, most of what goes on inside Jakarta's love hotels can hardly be labeled a family holiday or corporate retreat. But these dens of lust actually meet a widespread social demand: In a society that officially shuns pre-marital sex, the existence of these hotels is testimony to how frequently it is practiced. Known locally by the euphemisms *Hotel Enam Jam-an* ("six-hour hotels") or *Pondok Wisata* ("tourism spot"), love hotels actually began quite innocently as roadside transit motels for inter-city travelers. Today they are the refuge of choice for randy young things who live at home until marriage and in the meantime yearn for private moments away from mom and dad's watchful gaze. Extra-marital flings are also very common in a city where divorce is still frowned upon, so love hotels are frequently used for what's locally known as *BBS* (*Bobok-Bobok Siang*, or 'afternoon naps'). In fact, rooms are most likely to be fully booked on weekday afternoons at around two or three o'clock. All of this means that occupancy rates at these love nests far exceed those at the city's luxury tourist hotels – no doubt to the dismay of the Jakarta Tourism Promotion Board.

Privacy is taken seriously at love hotels. For starters, the nondescript rows of single-story blocks look nothing like ordinary hotels and are usually set back from the main road, concealed behind rows of tall shrubs. Anonymity is guarded from the start: your car is escorted into one of many personal parking bays with doors that slide shut behind you as soon as you drive in, so that nobody will recognize your battered old red Kijang jeep and spread vicious stories around the office the next day. The garage leads straight into the bedroom. Check-in is done on the spot and with little fuss: a trusty clerk appears at your door with clean towels, a fresh bar of soap, and a receipt for the Rp 120,000 (around $12) you'll be paying for a six-hour time block. Rooms are generally clean, simple affairs (ouch, bad pun). They are air-conditioned and equipped with a TV, mini-bar, and bedside menu offering meals and snacks from the 24-hour room service. The en-suite bathrooms usually boast see-through doors (if you've ended up in a love hotel, feigning shyness would seem besides the point). Deluxe rooms even include waterbeds, oversized bathtubs, free in-house porn on TV, and ornate ceiling mirrors. True palaces of good old-fashioned love.

MACET

EVER SINCE Indonesia's economic boom in the 1980s, bumper-to-bumper traffic has made the nation's capital a much cozier place. Jakarta's so-called town planners left little room for a solution – building property first and roads later. A subway system is thought to be almost impossible given the city's near-sea-level location (though for some reason grand plans are drawn up each year for an underground train anyway, only to be scrapped). A 3-in-1 regulation for rush hour commuter vehicles spawned a clever new source of employment for young Jakartans (see 'Road Jockeys' chapter) but did little to alleviate the gridlock thing.

Jakarta's notorious *macet* (pronounced "MAH-Chet") has a profound impact on day-to-day routine in the city, at the root of which lies the Indonesian concept of *jam karet* ('rubber time'). The utter unpredictability of gridlock makes showing up late or not showing up at all completely forgivable. *Macet* makes stated arrival times irrelevant, letting off the hook in a big way everyone from inept cabinet ministers to lazy pizza delivery boys. *Macet* hell – aptly termed *macet total* – is trying to leave the city on a long weekend during heavy monsoon rain. This was certainly the case in Jakarta on February 2, 2002: since 02-02-02 was considered an auspicious date, weddings were scheduled everywhere, creating traffic jams so extreme that many intended wedding guests ended up in gridlock overnight. The flow of city traffic eases slightly toward the end of each calendar month: when salaries start drying up and pay day is a while off, car owners can't always afford gasoline.

Macet is a self-sustaining economy, offering outstanding job opportunities to unemployed Jakartans: young men help agitated drivers perform U-turns; buskers shake bottle-cap instruments and scream horrific 'tunes'; and vendors sell everything from cigarettes to crystal horse statues – to a customer base that's quite literally captive. *Macet* also constitutes a rare outlet for rudeness and confrontation in largely Javanese Jakarta: whereas social convention doesn't allow you to snap at a useless clerk at the bank, stolen road rage moments let you aggressively overtake his wimpy motorbike at high speed with your big metal machine.

Macet is beautiful because Jakartans from very different walks of life feed off it in alarmingly similar ways. Just as our Guns n' Roses-inspired traffic light busker lines his pockets with small change, so too does the corrupt traffic cop, and ditto former president Soeharto's toll-road-owning kids. The rest of the population looks at Bangkok's swanky Skytrain system with desperate envy.

LESS FORTUNATE CITIES make do with parks, beaches, playgrounds, outdoor promenades or even stuffy cultural centers as the places where their residents meet and interact. Jakartans are far luckier. They have The Mall.

Malls are air-conditioned to bone-chilling extremes. Malls contain lots of bright glitzy things on display (not just dressed-to-kill teenaged girls, but actual retail merchandise, too). Malls have food courts galore and awful live bands and overflowing cineplexes. Malls have pricey cafes and noisy video arcades and trendy salons and obnoxious kiddy pageants. A few malls in Jakarta even have ice skating rinks. Most of all, malls are the place Jakartans go to see and be seen. Typical patrons include, but are not limited to: skateboard-toting teenagers; gossip-driven high society madams; business folks on power lunches; gay men on the prowl; soap opera stars on spending sprees; house maids with long grocery lists; uniformed nannies in hot pursuit of screaming brats; tourists hunting for Batik scarves and 'authentic' shadow puppets. In short, the reason nobody visits Ragunan Zoo in South Jakarta is because the human zoo inside the city's malls is far more colorful, involves no entrance charge, is air-conditioned, and offers plenty of underground parking.

Considering that for most Indonesians the past few years have been a period of *krismon*, or 'monetary crisis' (see 'Krismon' chapter), Jakarta's mega-malls are pretty darn busy. The most popular, Plaza Senayan, is a case study in just how immune a developing country's upper class can be to rough economic times. How else to explain the going rate for leasing space in this gleaming bastion of consumerism – about US$10,000 per month for a medium-sized shop? And still, the waiting list to secure any store space here at all is over six months long. Weekends at any popular Jakarta mall add a new twist to the idea of 'population density on Java', and are a test for anybody's patience: you will be forgiven for developing an urge to kick certain mall browsers for their slow, aimless strolling and wavering flight patterns in the shoulder-to-shoulder sea of human traffic.

MASSAGE CENTERS

IN RECENT YEARS massage centers have become almost as central to Jakarta existence as, say, petrol stations or local supermarkets. The concept is nothing new. Massage treatment is long-steeped in Indonesian culture, and remains an especially popular form of stress relief for stressed-out Jakartans. Most neighborhoods have their own 'roving' *tukang pijat* or *mbok* – usually an elderly man or woman boasting outrageously powerful hands and an impressive array of traditional oils for massaging customers in the comfort of their own homes. But yuppie lifestyle has meant more sophistication and diversity in the trade. The past few years has seen the mushrooming of trendy massage havens in the city center, complete with air-con, hot showers and even swanky Japanese eateries in the lobby.

Jakarta's most popular massage centers, like Bersih Sehat ('Clean & Healthy'), typically boast three huge floors of private booths where for the equivalent of $7 an hour, expert masseuses deliver one of the best shiatsu-style treatments this side of Yokohama. After a refreshing shower, the masseuse will throw you onto a treatment bed and proceed to grind your bones and muscles. She'll even walk all over your back and crack your spine with her bare heels – one of the scariest and most satisfying sensations imaginable. Don't try this at home. But back-trampling is optional, as is the Shiatsu variety of treatment. Instead, one can go for the 'traditional Indonesian' massage – the more familiar deep-rubbing-with-oil deal that feels great and is decidedly less risky.

Massage centers exist all over the city, but be forewarned that some of these establishments are staffed by masseuses that are suddenly a whole lot younger, wear curiously shorter uniforms and often happen to be drop-dead gorgeous. Following from this, the massages they give tend to be somewhat more 'creative' and for a generous tip they will perform all sorts of additional services. Definitely don't try *this* at home. It should be noted that such forms of creative treatment are offered even inside the health clubs of Jakarta's top international-chain hotels, but I won't mention names because it's a sensitive issue (Hi Tuti! Still working weekdays at the Continental?).

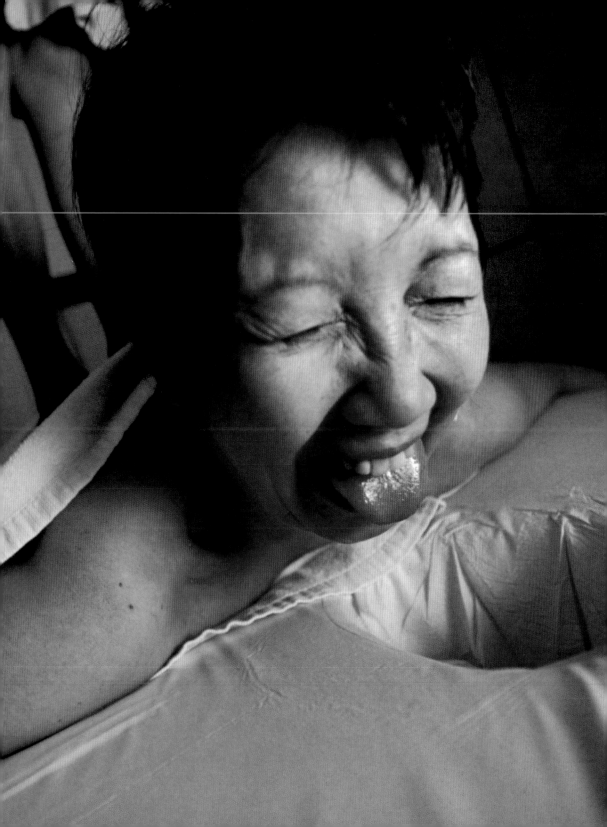

THE POLITICALLY CORRECT WAY to refer to Jakarta's chaos, petty crime, turf wars, mob rule and inter-ethnic hatred is to call the city a 'big cultural melting pot'. The melting pot approach views the city's populace as a smiling happy bunch of people, all grateful for the opportunity to celebrate their colorful diversity through a collective urban experience.

In a way, this isn't far from the truth. Indonesians from across the archipelago have always flocked to the bustling capital in search of new opportunities and the promise of big city prosperity. Each year after the Muslim Lebaran holiday season, around 250,000 migrants reckon Jakarta isn't full enough yet, and decide to hop on board. This may be an immigrant city, but one ethnic group, the *Betawi*, claims to be Jakarta's true natives. Wrong! Myth! The *Betawi* people are actually of mixed Sundanese, Javanese, Balinese, Malay, Chinese and even Arab and Dutch descent. And since *Betawi* only emerged in late 19th-century Batavia, other ethnic groups can claim an earlier foothold in the city.

But never mind all that. An unwritten, highly stereotypical occupation code exists underneath Jakarta's cultural confusion, and it goes something like this:

You are an upper-middle class Indonesian of Chinese descent, and therefore work for your family's trading company; you place legal affairs in the hands of your attorney, an ethnic Batak from North Sumatra; he recently even helped you purchase a plot of land behind your house from an ethnic *Betawi* Jakartan, who owned the property for three generations but needed the money to go on *Haj* pilgrimage to Mecca, at the advice of his soft-spoken neighborhood cleric, who's from East Java; meanwhile, your housekeeper Inem, from Central Java, said she thinks your rich neighbor – a mafia boss originally from Ambon in the Maluku islands – can get your car fixed for free by a thug from Flores island who runs a garage in the Tanah Abang district; this sounds like a good idea, because ever since the car trouble began you've been unable to take your wife to tacky hotel lounges to hear her favorite singers, usually Christians from Ambon, Lake Toba, or Manado in North Sulawesi. You could go by taxi, but you'd have to deal with a driver from Cirebon, West Java, who has yet to figure out his way around the city since moving here a mere 19 years ago; or you could take a Metro Mini bus, but the Batak driver, Batak conductor and Batak pickpocket wouldn't be nearly as classy as your Batak lawyer, and you might mess up the new suit made by your tailor, that cheap little bastard from Padang in West Sumatra; you thought of buying a new car with an advance from your loan shark, who is of course from Tasikmalaya in West Java, but his wife, a former bar girl, just left him so she could re-marry for the fourth time, because she is ethnic Sundanese.

Now you know.

95

METRO MINI

JAKARTA IS A VAST city where getting from point A to B can be a grand odyssey in itself. Its more privileged residents get to negotiate traffic from the comfort (or discomfort) of their own cars. Those who are vehicle-deficient yet can afford to part with just over Rp 3,000 (around 30 cents) per trip, might opt for one of those large Patas AC buses. The rest of the herd have to settle for being squashed, sardine-like, in a Metro Mini.

The Metro Mini (or one of its competitors, like Kopaja or Koantas Bima) is widely considered the bane of Jakarta's roads, its loud orange hue making it seem like the bajaj's obnoxious older brother. The faults attributed to it are as numerous as Sukarno's wives: there's the general unpleasantness of the buses themselves, all dilapidated and spewing thick exhaust; the incessant stopping to pick up and drop off passengers wherever they please, hardly ever halting at actual bus stops; and the kenek (conductors) cram in as many people as possible, always insisting there's "still plenty more space" when it's blatantly clear the people already inside are experiencing significant respiratory problems.

But people have places to go and so they acquiesce, even if it means hanging on for dear life from the always-open doorframe. The way the predominantly Batak drivers (see 'Melting Pot' chapter) weave through traffic would surely give Michael Schumacher a coronary. It's all about ngejar setoran ('accumulating fares') you see: The faster they go, the more fares they can rack up in a day for their boss. On the flipside, they won't even budge until the bus is overloaded, holding up roadside traffic all the while. And beware if it's nighttime and your bus is suddenly quite empty; odds are you'll get shunted onto another bus just a kilometer or two short of your destination, while your previous transport heads back to its pool.

Then there's the credibility of the drivers themselves. Occasionally a bus will stop somewhere that doesn't even remotely resemble a terminal, and the driver will climb off only to be replaced by some dubious-looking fellow. Since none of them wear uniforms, your well-being is now in the hands of someone who for all you know hasn't even mastered the tricycle. Driver recklessness has led to numerous tragedies, like one particularly regrettable plunge into the Sunter River, which drowned all the passengers. More common disasters involve Metro Minis crashing into people. When this occurs, the surrounding populace will waste no time in trashing the bus and setting fire to it, along with the driver and kenek if they haven't already escaped (see 'Street Justice' chapter).

And then there are the usual incidents, like being hijacked by warring high school gangs on a joy ride into enemy territory, or being bled dry by friendly neighborhood pickpockets. Keeping a low profile is therefore crucial when riding a Metro Mini. All things considered, cattle-class train can seem like first class transportation by comparison. At least you avoid traffic…

MONAS

IT IS TEMPTING to refer to Indonesia's National Monument by its endearing and enduring popular term, 'Sukarno's Final Erection' – but I won't, as this could be considered disrespectful to the country's statue-loving, womanizing first president. Monas is short for *Monumen Nasional*, and lies in what should be the lungs of Jakarta – a large park surrounded by traffic fumes and political demonstrations.

Monas was first commissioned by Sukarno in 1961, but wasn't officially opened until 1975 by his successor and nemesis, President Soeharto. The 132-meter tower is made of Italian marble and capped by a glittering bronze flame gilded with 35 kilos of gold leaf. Far more impressive than the structure itself is the compulsive symbolism inherent in it: The date of Indonesia's declaration of independence, 17/8/1945, is incorporated into practically every nook and cranny. The lower terrace measures 45 by 45 meters and sits 17 meters above ground level; 17 steps lead to the tower's entrance, and its tunnel is 45 meters long; even the surrounding fence boasts a very patriotic 1,945 pillars; whether or not the tower's opening hours (08:00-17:00) are but an extension of the same obsession remains to be seen.

Underneath the imposing structure is a museum where cool dioramas depict watershed moments in Indonesian history through the eyes of the paranoid Soeharto regime – arguably the greatest re-writers of history ever. The dark, cavernous Soviet-style hall that houses the museum is far too big for its stated purpose. It should instead be used for giant raves. It could be re-named the *Monas-try of Sound*. The acoustics would be spectacular.

But for all the nationalist imagery going on here, Monas Park can still be a great place for a stroll. In the early morning it is dotted with *Tai Chi* groups doing their concentrated daily workout. In the afternoon, *delman* horse carriages ferry families and young couples around the cobblestone plaza that circles the monument. And the street market that unfolds here each night is typical of the bustling *pasar kaget* bazaars found in cities across Indonesia. Everything is for sale: inflatable Teletubbies and imitation name-brand shoes; cacophonous alarm clocks and bulk shampoo; flimsily assembled disco lights and even flimsier cassette players; bumper stickers bearing Islamic slogans or images of cult rock band Slank; cheap, colorful children's clothing and budget accessories for the car; cotton candy and fried tofu; prayer mats and bed linen; fake Rolexes and spicy fried rice.

KNOWN BY THE LOCAL acronym *OKB* (*Orang Kaya Baru*, or 'new rich people') Jakarta's New Rich class comprises industry executives, top military brass, young entrepreneurs, entertainment stars of dubious talent, small-time politicians who've suddenly made it big, and children of the Old Rich who've found new and interesting things to do with daddy's money. They originate from different worlds, but all seem to have two things in common. First, their lifestyle has not been affected (and may have even been improved) by the ongoing monetary crisis; second, like New Rich folks everywhere, they seem not to know what to do with all the money they've accumulated and indulge in things that us common folk – in our badly-concealed jealousy – like to dismiss as 'tasteless'.

It's an enviable lifestyle, sort of. Their Maseratis and S-Class Mercedes cruise effortlessly through Jakarta's traffic alongside sputtering *bajaj* and guitar-wielding beggars; they hold executive memberships at the city's most decadent health clubs; and their grandiose mansions are sometimes big enough to house the entire population of a medium-size slum. Then there's the obsession with imported name-brand fashion accessories (although some rich kids could use a few lessons in how to mix and match them with greater finesse).

A few immutable laws govern the behavior of Jakarta's New Rich. First, the more something costs, the more they'll want to buy it. Second, since status is intrinsically linked to possessing the very latest gadgets, they will never, ever wait for the price of a trendy new gadget to drop before buying it. Third, they shrewdly build relationships within the murky, corrupt world of Jakarta politics and adapt to the winds of change; in the past decade, for instance, many of the city's *nouveau riche* underwent a magical reincarnation from enthusiastic Soeharto-era benefactors to vocal supporters of the now-trendy reform movement.

Jakarta's Affluent Young Things are usually educated in places like Singapore, Australia or the U.S.A. They like to travel, but normally to destinations such as Sydney or Hong Kong, where their overseas adventure involves hooking up with other New Rich friends to do something I've always wanted to do: compare the relative virtues of their cities' top luxury hotel restaurants. For Jakarta's jet-setting class the nearest department store is Tangs in Singapore, although a truly serious shopping spree would necessitate a Business Class trip to New York.

Upon return from university, New Rich kids either join the family business or branch out to become 'entrepreneurs'. This is when life gets really sweet, because 'work' suddenly means opening stylish new bars, restaurants and galleries – an enviable career, to say the least. Eventually, their photos start appearing on the party pages of *Tatler* magazine, which they pretend to be embarrassed about, but which really means they've finally come of age in Jakarta high society.

101

IF ONE THING stands in stark contrast to Jakarta's fast pace, and is its natural antidote, it is the delicate art of *nongkrong*. The official dictionary definition of the verb is 'sitting around and not working,' but in colloquial Bahasa Indonesia translates as something like 'hanging out'. The act can be performed by squatting on the roadside, sitting on the front steps of one's house, lying in a hammock, sitting atop a bunch of parked motorbikes, or even leaning against a railing in the shopping mall. Classic *nongkrong* is done wearing flip-flops and smoking a pungent *kretek* clove cigarette (see 'Kretek' chapter). *Nongkrong* is a means without an end. The purpose of *nongkrong* is…*nongkrong*. And it is not a fleeting, five-minute activity. *Nongkrong* must be long and drawn out, with absolutely no sense of urgency and no agenda whatsoever. If someone is doing something else like eating, for instance, they are not *nongkrong*, they are eating. Similarly, if they have to be somewhere in half an hour, they are not *nongkrong* either.

The average American reportedly spends three-and-a-half hours in front of the TV each day; the same can be said for many Jakartans with *nongkrong*. But Indonesians love TV too, and incredibly, some Jakartans manage to devote nearly this much time to both *nongkrong* AND watching TV.

The traditional image of *nongkrong* is of an unemployed slum-dweller hanging out by the roadside with his friends, but *nongkrong* culture went 'up-market' in the mid-1980s when it was adopted by a generation of young, upwardly mobile Jakartans. The city's youth probably took their cue from the outrageously popular radio serial 'Catatan Si Boy', which inspired many teenage trends at that time. For lack of shopping malls in those pre-boom years, their *nongkrong* venue of choice was the hip and teeming Jalan Melawai in South Jakarta (see 'Blok M' chapter).

OJEK

MOTORBIKE TAXIS, known as *ojek,* are arguably the most efficient way to get around in gridlock-prone Jakarta. The paying passenger nervously clutches the back tail bar of the bike while the driver weaves through traffic at lightening speed, slowing down only for red lights (optional) or collisions (disturbingly frequent). It's the way many children get to school, clerks to the office and housewives to the market and back. Women wearing dresses or skirts normally sit sidewise across the back seat – probably best for everyone that way. At red lights on main roads in Jakarta, a sea of rumbling motorbikes inevitably lead the pack, having cunningly pulled ahead of the far less agile cars and buses stuck behind them.

The law says motorbike drivers must wear helmets at all times, but *ojek* drivers don't usually take this interesting regulation too seriously. The 'helmets' they reluctantly wear tend to be thin, flimsy things with broken straps. Round, colorful, plastic objects flying Ewok-like through the air are consequently a pretty common hazard on Jakarta roads. More worrying still is when the *ojek* driver decides to turn right back around and retrieve his helmet - against the flow of oncoming traffic…

Best of all, no regulations govern the operation of *ojek* in Jakarta, meaning practically anyone can operate an *ojek* just about anywhere. The on-again-off-again ban on three-wheeled *bajaj* in the city (see 'Bajaj' chapter) has meant *ojek* drivers can cash in on all those extra customers. Some folks even have a 'regular' neighborhood *ojek* driver on standby with a handphone (see 'Handphones' chapter) to shuttle them to work or on errands around the city.

NO TRAFFIC LIGHT JUNCTION or public bus route in Jakarta would be complete without a handful of musical street buskers known as *pengamen*. Many of these young entertainers are bona fide homeless street kids who literally sing for their supper. Others are bored, unemployed youngsters with roofs over their heads for whom street busking is a means of extra income. Either way, the *pengamen* world is a powerful Jakarta sub-culture in its own right, with rules and a language of its own. The term itself is thought to come from the 'amin' or 'amen' often uttered when they beg for money or recite a prayer.

Given that music is their bread and butter, a disturbingly high percentage of *pengamen* appear to be 'musically challenged' - much to the dismay of anyone stuck in a car at a traffic light during rush hour. Often, the entire two-minute duration of a red light can elapse before one recognizes the particular song a *pengamen* is trying to croon. *Pengamen* tend to be ruthless guitar-abusers, too. The concept of a chord is alien to many, and strings seem to pop loose with the same violent gusto that they are 'strummed'.

But serious *pengamen* are a different story altogether. They are a talented, organized bunch. They ply air-conditioned bus routes, entertaining passengers with two-and three-part harmonies, masterful guitar playing, and an impressive 'stage presence'. On a good day they'll bag as much as Rp 100,000 ($10), on a bad one about half that.

The musical instruments they use similarly follow a certain hierarchy; the *pengamen* musical food chain starts with the *krecek* (a small wooden contraption with rattling bottle caps at one end) and progresses to the tamborine, yukelele and finally guitar.

An estimated 4000 *pengamen* work the city's buses and traffic junctions, but this figure includes only kids that play a proper instrument, boast a repertoire of at least five tunes, and sing for a living. The figure is much higher when *pengamen*-wannabes – the ones that stand zombie-like, managing only to scream and clap – are taken into account.

But *pengamen* life is no walk in the park. Dangers loom everywhere, from police raids to bullying by local *preman* thugs and even violent assaults by desperate petty thieves. 'Turf wars' are a regular feature of life as a street singer; traffic intersections are carefully demarcated by different *pengamen* groups, and protected with great zeal by mafia 'landlords'.

Local authorities periodically crack down on *pengamen* activity, usually by rounding up the youngsters and taking them to a 'Social Center' (i.e. jail) in West Jakarta, releasing them the next morning when a family member shows up to cough up 'bail' to the tune of about Rp 50,000 (around $5). 107

PIGEON RACING

FORGET DOG RACES or cockfighting. In Jakarta, pigeon racing is where it's all at. The hobby probably has a lot to do with the Javanese obsession with birds (rare birds, singing birds, mythological birds, you name it). Every Sunday at the now-defunct Kemayoran airfield and other locations around Jakarta, the *kalangan burung* ('bird people') exhibit their skills by racing their prize pigeons for the ultimate reward, namely, the respect of rivals. Oh, and maybe some cash, and a new motorbike if it happens to be the Independence Day commemoration races.

The process of training champions-to-be is usually long and painstaking. Male racing pigeons can be bred at home, but most often they are purchased somewhere in Central Java. They must be carefully selected based on very specific criteria, primarily favorable physical traits and the right lineage. Like hillbillies, inbred pigeons are frowned upon. A particularly fine pigeon can fetch up to Rp 3 million (around $300). The search for female mate then commences, and is probably the most crucial phase of race pigeon preparation.

Mating?! Here's how it works: During the race, sexy female pigeons are held in the hands of pigeon jockeys at the finish line some four kilometers away, as bait to lure the males. Put bluntly, the whole thing is set up so that the horniest male ends up winning. Hence the importance of the mating process; the male and female need to be so head-over-claws in love that the male will want to leave his competition in the proverbial dust for some good ol' lovin'. The human equivalent would be heading straight home from the office instead of stopping at the bar for drinks.

But competitors can sabotage rivals' efforts by dangling other females along the Ancol-Kemayoran route, hoping to throw the males off their stride by luring them aside for a quickie (another human behavior parallel). Distracted pigeons are often captured by local children and held for ransom — accepted practice in the cutthroat pigeon-racing world and a form of one-upping the competition. But a pigeon's woes don't end with the fear of being kidnapped. Sometimes an over-eager pigeon will descend towards the finish line at such lightning speed that he'll fail to break in time and crash head-on into the colored structure where the female awaits, killing himself in the process. It's an incredibly romantic gesture, if a bit messy.

For purposes of recognition from afar, pigeons sometimes receive a coat of bright paint, or get a whistle attached to their tail. If ever on a Sunday you hear a loud shrieking sound overhead, it's probably a restless male pigeon jetting home for some much-anticipated nookie.

PIRACY

IN ITS HEYDAY, Southeast Asia was the maritime crossroads of the world, a celebrated playground for seafaring pirates who hopped famously from island to island to loot and kill and…yes, even trade. Today's pirates demonstrate equally ambitious business flair, but are more likely to be found at a street stall in downtown Jakarta hawking fake Ralph Lauren shirts, imitation designer handbags or counterfeit CDs.

Piracy in Asia has become an awful headache for the WTO, branded clothing designers, chambers of commerce, major record labels and Hollywood film studios, but in Jakarta it is a central part of the day-to-day economy. In fact, most Jakartans wouldn't dream of buying an original product at an original price. They opt for look-alike copies (known as *bajakan*) produced either locally or in similarly innovative countries like China and Malaysia. Original DVD films, for instance, can carry a hefty Rp 250,000 (around $25) price tag, whilst near-perfect copies cost just Rp 40,000 (around $4). Cheaper still are movies on pirated VCD (Video Compact Discs), available at any market for as little as Rp 7,000 (around 70 cents). And, while authentic Armani jeans fetch around Rp 1.5 million (around $150) at an official boutique, a fake can be had for as little as one-tenth of that price. These days, global counterfeiting is estimated to cost European businesses as much as $50 billion per year.

Trading in counterfeit goods is of course illegal, but Jakarta police haven't been particularly zealous in combating the mischievous practice. Vendors of pirated goods in the city's Chinatown know the reason they are allowed to operate is that too many people – including police and municipal officials – get a handsome cut. Sellers are regularly visited by both the mafia and the authorities (don't confuse the two!) and expected to fork over generous sums in 'protection money'. When payments aren't quite satisfactory, the police or municipality will launch a highly publicized 'raid', with the double aim of creating the rare impression that they are doing their job, and teaching those stingy vendors a lesson in generosity. Even after particularly violent raids, the resilient vendors are back up and operating within a day or two.

EVERY CITY HAS its affluent neighborhoods, and Jakarta is no exception. Areas like Menteng, Kebayoran, Pondok Indah and Kemang are home to many of Jakarta's wealthiest residents.

Sometimes it's 'old money' – landowners from pre-independence days, cronies from the New Order regime boom years, or folks well-connected enough to have had a stake in some of Indonesia's leading conglomerates. Their houses tend to be spacious and very comfortable, but somehow bear the simplicity of Old Jakarta – traditional kitchens; airy living rooms with high ceilings and large ceiling fans; teak wood or rattan furniture; lush gardens.

Like 'new money' people everywhere, Jakarta's New Rich (see 'New Rich' chapter) seem determined to test the limits of both their purchasing power and of publicly accepted taste. In Jakarta's southern suburbs – Pondok Indah in particular – they build gargantuan new homes that from the main road look a bit like badly constructed spaceships or poor reproductions of Disney-style palaces. In short, garish in just about every way. If you are ever feeling sorry for yourself for being poor, take a stroll along Pondok Indah's main road, and see the kind of home you have been spared.

The entrance façade sometimes carries the family's initials in huge gold letter plates; the front courtyard might contain a pair of life-sized ceramic statues of Pegasus; the gleaming marble-laid living room is the size of a small stadium; chandeliers typically weigh two hundred kilos and house enough light bulbs to illuminate a casino; the swimming pool will usually be lined with spitting fountains; the children's bedrooms are often the work of a specialist interior designer and the kids' beds are shaped like racing cars or medieval castles. Check these houses out. They epitomize post-modern kitsch. But most impressive of all, real people with real choices actually *choose* to live in them.

115

SPARTAN BAMBOO HUTS called *posko* are where urban space and local politics come colorfully together in Jakarta's inner neighborhoods. Short for *pos komando* ('command post'), they first appeared as a grassroots response by *kampung* (urban village) communities to acute economic need at the height of Indonesia's 1997 monetary crisis (see 'Krismon' chapter). The posts served as strategic distribution points for *sembako* - basic rations like rice and cooking oil - and aimed to instill a sense of local security in an increasingly unstable political environment. The principle behind the *posko* was the much-celebrated Javanese idea of *gotong royong*, or 'community self-help'.

But during the 1999 general election campaign, *posko* were transformed into strategic political footholds, mainly by the PDI-P party of presidential candidate Megawati Soekarnoputri. The flimsy structures began acquiring the trappings of a personality cult, and images of Megawati and her legendary father, Sukarno, loomed large over the entrances to *posko* everywhere; it was here that neighborhood party branches mobilized for rallies and distributed campaign leaflets; and often, usually well into the night, the posts became a new space for political debate, or just innocent guitar playing. When the *posko* trend was at its peak, over 5,000 of them are known to have existed in Jakarta alone.

Eventually, the mostly red-colored *posko* were slapped with a thick coat of white paint by the authorities, in an effort to de-politicize the whole phenomenon. Most *posko* have been dormant for some time now. But many still spring back to life if, when and where a political cause arises. Either way, a neglected bamboo structure with torn red flags is now a Jakarta landmark on just about any neighborhood side street.

117

THE WORD *PUNCAK*, meaning 'peak', ostensibly describes the mountainous landscape of Jakarta's favorite weekend out-of-town getaway. But 'peak' equally describes the traffic situation leading up to the hilly resort from Friday morning through Sunday night of just about any week. Stressed out by life in the big city, members of Jakarta's middle-upper class delight in lining up their Toyota *Kijang* jeeps for a stop-and-go, bumper-to-bumper trip that can take up to five hours to cover the mere 70 km stretch of road. An extra day in Puncak is needed just to recover from the nerve-wracking journey.

Once up there and tucked away safely in one of thousands of tranquil villas overlooking lush green valleys (or overlooking other tranquil villas), the air is cool and sweet. Frogs and crickets supply a natural soundtrack, while flowers, shrubs and tea plantations complete the local landscape. The serenity has meant that many Jakarta-based corporations maintain holiday properties in Puncak – really just lung-cleansing retreats for over-polluted executives. A variety of religious and cultural groups have set up oases here too, making for a rather unlikely mix of organizational hideaways in the area. Along one mountainous stretch, for instance, sits a Nichiren Buddhist temple, a Sufi meditation center, a golf course built by Tommy Soeharto (notorious son of the ex-president), a mosque run by an Imam who's also a lawyer for the fundamentalist Laskar Jihad movement, and the Indonesian Police Education Center (which cynics would claim is an oxymoron).

The main road winding through Puncak is peppered with a vast assortment of 'amusements' for weekend holiday goers, each more obnoxious than the next: tacky restaurants with offensive music and mediocre food; sleazy discothèques with sleazy bar girls; a miniature safari park; love hotels advertised by roadside touts as 'Villas', where women are included in the room rate; karaoke bars that cut violently through the hilltop silence; and the mountain crest of Puncak Pass itself – indeed the peak of tackiness for its many young lovers walking hand in hand, stealing romantic moments alongside overpriced souvenir stalls and cement animal statues.

INTERESTING ATTEMPTS ARE MADE in tourist promotion literature to equate Asian cities with romantic places back in Europe. Bangkok and even Banjarmasin, for instance, are sometimes dubbed 'Venices of the East' for their canal systems. It's a stretch, but a vague similarity exists. Jakarta has canals, but doesn't even merit a nickname like 'Cleveland of the East', because these narrow waterways carry the kind of sewage and waste that make the smell of durian seem like Issey Miyake perfume by comparison.

Jakarta's nearly 400 km of waterways are a strange thing. For most of each year the city's canals (called *sungai* and *kali*) are pathetic little streams whose main function appears to be transporting waste from one neighborhood to the next. But when torrential monsoon rains arrive, these tributaries suddenly become gushing rivers that flood homes and highways.

It shouldn't be this way. The absence of proper city planning, a lack of green belt areas, and improper building development are major causes of these periodic flooding debacles (oh - and those rains have something to with it too). Everyone knows that besides the annual wet season downpour, a devastating 'bonus round' of rain is delivered to the city approximately every five years. But to date no city administration has had the foresight to spend the necessary time and money on building proper drainage canals on the city's outskirts. So about twice each decade Jakarta becomes a real-life Waterworld, at great human cost.

The last time this occurred was in early 2002. Dozens of residents were killed and thousands made homeless by rains that washed away entire slums, turned highway underpasses into dangerous water tunnels, and saw bewildered tourists evacuated from a submerged Regent Hotel on plastic blue laundry crates. It was a tragic time – an example of Jakarta quite literally drowning in official incompetence. But it was also a memorable period in which the city's residents banded together in an admirable display of mutual help. Emergency relief posts sprang up in neighborhoods everywhere, and citizens from all walks of life donated money, food and shelter. For a few short weeks, and in the face of calamity and chaos, the city seemed to find its soul. Where government failed, ordinary Jakartans managed to stay afloat, assert their own power and take charge of their fate once again.

'RIVERS' & FLOODS

121

BY CREATING a 3-in-1 rush hour traffic regulation along the city's main arteries, municipal authorities created a viable new profession for unemployed youth, and a whole new source of bribes for municipal law enforcement officials. To discourage excessive volumes of traffic, private vehicles using Jakarta's main roads during morning and evening rush hour must carry a minimum of three passengers. The regulation did little to solve the city's traffic problem. Instead, entrepreneurial 'road jockeys' - mostly young boys - improvised by offering to hop on as 'passengers' in cars that don't meet the 3-in-1 criteria. Some jockeys are even mothers toting infants – the 'value pack' of the jockey world because they count as two.

The going rate for a jockey 'run' is Rp 2,000 (about 20 cents). Jockeys line the roadside and hop into private vehicles immediately before the 3-in-1 zone begins. They hop out again just about anywhere within the zone, since drivers are theoretically allowed to drop car-poolers off at destinations inside the central business district. A jockey run can therefore be a hop-in-hop-out journey of 200 meters, with the exercise repeated by the same jockey perhaps ten times in a single morning. Simple yet ingenious, and certainly not a bad deal for just sitting in the back of an air-con car watching a rich dude drive himself to work. Drivers plying the same route to work each morning often begin to know specific jockeys and will have a 'regular' they like to use. The only obstacle in this whole game: municipal street superintendents that roam the regulated zone and try to nab the young jockeys as they hop out of cars. If it all sounds like a badly designed video game, that's pretty much how it feels to anyone involved, too. Jockeys unlucky enough to be caught are hauled off to the municipal 'Social Center' in West Jakarta and kept behind bars until a relative shows up with Rp 100,000 (around $10) to set them free. Then they hit the road again.

123

IN WESTERN SOCIETY, hair salon treatments, spas and other beauty-related indulgences carry the connotation of luxury, even decadence. Not so in Jakarta. Whether due to the city's stress levels or because of Javanese traditions that far predate modern-day traffic and pollution, spoiling oneself frequently and thoroughly in a salon is regarded more as a God-given right than shameful hedonism.

To be sure, 'down time' in a salon is in no way limited to Jakarta's elite: even the city's slums boast scaled-down versions of beauty and hair salons – usually small wooden huts with a chair, some extremely backdated fashion mags and a hand-painted 'salon' sign out front. Here, for around Rp 8,000 (80 cents), a vegetable seller at the local market can come in from a long day of haggling and spoil herself silly for a good hour or so.

Meanwhile, Jakarta's high society ladies will fork over considerably more moolah for a few hours of fun in decidedly more decadent surroundings. (Note: this sort of outing is often sponsored by hubby's Platinum Card, in which case the day becomes even more enjoyable, involves a few narcissistic but giggly friends and incredible pre- and post-salon shopping possibilities). A basic hairdo at a fashionable salon can cost Rp 200,000 (around $20), while a heavenly few hours of manicure, pedicure, facial, creambath and massage will easily add up to Rp 1 million (around $100) or more. But for this sum you are assured of being treated by the finest gay hairdressers in town and sharing hair spray and Perrier with some of the city's most superficial celebrities, who with puzzled glimpses will look over and wonder whether they know you or whether they should *get* to know you.

A few remarks on the famous Indonesian 'creambath'. First, it's not a bath in cream, or anything quite so sensual. It is basically a thorough hair wash followed by a head, neck and shoulder massage using an herbal conditioning cream. Eventually, with the cream fully rubbed in, a steamer is applied so that the cream seeps into the pores and revitalizes the hair and scalp. A heavenly neck and shoulder massage by a magical pair of hands can mean the difference between a miserable week and a great one.

KNOWN LOCALLY as *kampung kumuh*, Jakarta's urban slums are an eyesore the government would prefer you didn't see. Slum dwellers are regularly evicted to make way for toll roads, golf courses, canals, stadiums, shopping malls, or simply a more pleasant view. In the Ramadan holiday period in 2001 alone, an estimated 35,000 slum dwellers were evicted from their roadside shacks - often violently - by municipal authorities. This policy follows the rationale that these makeshift huts represent illegal housing, and a huge allocation for eviction initiatives exists within the municipality's official budget. Some evictees were offered humiliating 're-settlement compensation' to the tune of Rp 100,000 (around $10). Others received nothing at all.

Possibly the most striking impression of Jakarta's slums is how closely they reside to shimmering skyscrapers and luxury housing, often in the very heart of the city. You can probably guess who lived in the area first. Jakarta's Central Business District (see 'Golden Triangle' chapter) is now a curious juxtaposition of rich and poor that has yuppie executives looking down from high-rise office windows onto landscapes of ramshackle huts and open sewage. The bizarre contradiction often seems to go unnoticed by yuppie and slum dweller alike. Spirited local NGOs such as the Urban Poor Consortium are active in representing slum dwellers' interests and in trying to close Jakarta's painful socio-economic gap. But these organizations are engaged in an uphill battle and regularly face resistance by political interest groups and the authorities.

127

STATUES

UNFORTUNATELY, government-commissioned statues of dubious taste have to a great extent defined Jakarta's aesthetic landscape. Most of these bear testimony to the 1960s' and 70s' obsession with national pride, driven initially by the flamboyant president Sukarno, and later by his equally ambitious successor, Soeharto.

In reality, these odd sculptures evoke mockery more often than any sort of heartfelt pride. Suffice it to note their nicknames: the *Semangat Pemuda*, or 'Spirit of Youth', statue (pictured here) on the southern end of Jalan Sudirman is lovingly known as 'Pizza Man' or sometimes 'Hotplate Harry'. No explanation necessary.

Similarly, the *Selamat Datang*, or 'Welcome' statue at Hotel Indonesia roundabout, which depicts a young man and woman cheerfully holding hands, is referred to as 'Donnie & Marie' or 'Hansel & Gretel'. (Note: student protesters love to climb to the top of this thing in an effort to hang political banners. To date, no one has been killed falling off, but a few have broken legs. It's a stunt that drives police officers crazy.)

The last of Sukarno's statues, the 1965 *Dirgantara*, is known as the 'Seven-Up Statue' because of the odd shape of its base. The *Monumen Pembebasan Irian Barat*, or 'Free West Irian' monument at Banteng Square, depicts a man breaking free of his chains. But Australians sometimes call it 'The Howzat Man' because it looks like someone appealing for a dismissal during a game of cricket.

STEMPEL & SPANDUK

MISSION: You are the acting Deputy Chairman on the Sub-Committee for Utilities and Maintenance (SCUM) of your neighborhood residents' council, and an important meeting is planned for next week. You will use the occasion to ratify a change to the group's acronym (this was finally agreed upon after months of drawn-out debate by a special Sub-Committee for Acronym Modification, known as SCAM). As a result, you will need to get a new set of rubber stamps made up with the modified name and logo. You also want to advertise the meeting at strategic points around the neighborhood, so that your wife, your mistress, and your mistress's good-for-nothing husband will all be impressed by what an influential guy you've become lately. Where do you turn?

Luckily, Jakarta is full of tiny street side *spanduk* and *stempel* vendors that produce inexpensive, custom-made banners and rubber stamps at lightning speed.

Spanduk, basically large cloth banners, are in huge demand in Jakarta for three main reasons. First, they are needed at a moment's notice for the many political demonstrations staged in the capital each week (see 'Demo' chapter). Next, banners are a popular form of local advertising, for everything from upcoming pop concerts to evening computer courses. Finally, colorful *spanduk* adorn the front of nearly every roadside food stall in the city. These tend to carry highly animated depictions of chickens (usually still full-feathered and smiling), catfish (often looking a bit downtrodden) and giant prawns (mostly with beautiful eyes and surprisingly thoughtful expressions).

Stempel are essentially custom-made rubber stamps. These, too, are in great demand, both as fuel for Indonesia's notorious bureaucracy and to symbolize the long-held reputation of the country's parliament. The existence of *stempel* stalls facilitates forgery and corruption, as basically anyone can order any sort of stamp overnight and at very little cost; creating impressive letterheads or receipt forms has never been simpler! People with less sinister intentions can order rubber stamps as a great gift for kids. Just check that the ink is non-toxic and doesn't end up all over the batik sofa upholstery.

Stempel and *spanduk* dudes also make a whole variety of other things to order, like license plates (car thieves take note!) and signs for shops and offices. Stalls are scattered all over the city, but true Jakarta *stempel* territory is along the bustling commercial street of Bendungan Hilir, just off Jalan Sudirman.

STREET JUSTICE

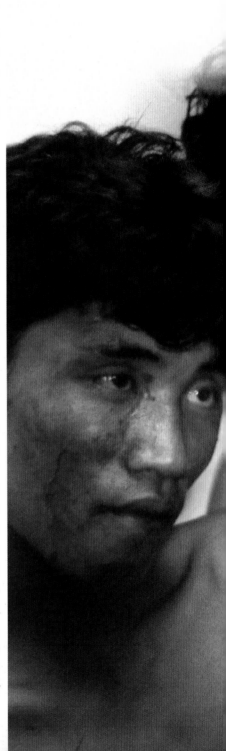

WHAT IS IT that suddenly transforms otherwise friendly neighborhood folks into a violent crowd that mercilessly clobbers an unarmed person to death? Perhaps it's a general absence of law and order in these politically unstable times; or a corrupt criminal justice system that's perceived never to hand out justice at all; or maybe it's economic hardship that drives ordinary people to unthinkable acts. Whatever the reason, Jakarta is suddenly a very dark and unfriendly place when it comes to mob lynching incidents known as *pengadilan jalanan*, or 'street justice'.

The unfortunate 'victim' usually began the day as a mischievous petty thief. He stole a chicken out of someone's courtyard, clothing off a laundry line, a motorbike parked in a back alley, or even just a plate of dried fish from a neighborhood market. Bad move. Local residents caught him in the act, word spread quickly around the block, and to cries of "Thief! Thief!" a vengeful mob galvanized around the terrified criminal to execute an immediate 'sentence'. If he was lucky, the mob beat him senseless but he lived to tell the tale; more likely, however, our hapless chicken thief was doused in kerosene and set alight, and is with us no more. (Such was the fate of the young car thieves being beaten here with a motorcycle helmet. They were never seen again.)

In recent years, instances of citizens taking the law into their own hands have grown worryingly frequent in Jakarta. Economic hardship stemming from the monetary crisis that began 1997 (see 'Krismon' chapter), and the collapse of authoritarian rule in 1998 combined to create an atmosphere of lawlessness on the street. Law enforcement officers are notorious for their reluctance to intervene, even if at the scene of a public lynching. Few such cases are ever investigated, and government officials do not even bother recording statistics on vigilante justice. But city tabloids continue to run gruesome stories about public beatings on a weekly basis, and it is estimated that in Greater Jakarta alone, hundreds of thieves are 'executed' in this manner each year. One commentator put it this way: Under authoritarianism, Indonesian society had "order without freedom," whereas under democracy it now has "freedom without order."

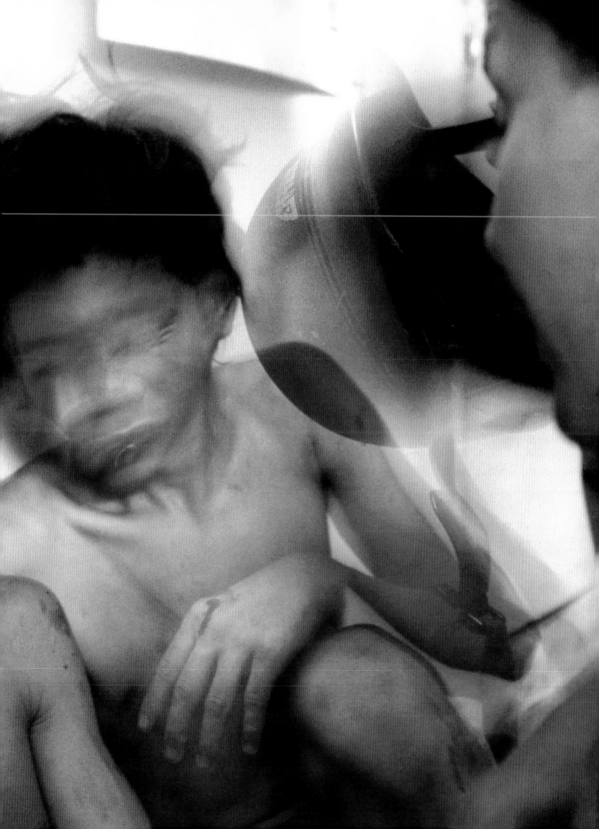

SWEATSHOPS

I REMEMBER an alarming statistic from *Harpers* magazine in 1992, which stated that it would take an ordinary Nike factory worker in Java more than 44,900 years to earn what celebrity basketball star Michael Jordan earned annually in endorsement fees from the very same company. Sometimes sensationalist numbers can spark important debates.

Jakarta's industrial belt consists of the suburbs of Bogor, Tangerang, and Bekasi (which make up the 'Bo', the 'Ta' and the 'Bek' in Jabotabek, the local term for Greater Jakarta). Botabek is home to hundreds of factories manufacturing products for companies that are household names in the West – shoes for Nike, clothing for The Gap, electronics for Sony, etc. Spokespersons for these companies argue that this is the bright side of globalization, because these factories provide hundreds of thousands of jobs for young Indonesians.

But it's difficult to spend a month in Jakarta without hearing about a workers' strike, trade union action, or an NGO complaint about the 'sweatshops' of Botabek. Factories here have become the regular focus of major international anti-sweatshop campaigns.

The term 'sweatshop' evokes images of hot, sweaty factories with hundreds of workers crammed into small, dark spaces, working around the clock without a break and earning 20 cents a day. Or barefoot ten-

machines and working eighteen-hour days on slave wages.

In reality, sweatshops in Botabek are not quite so bleak, but they certainly exist. A typical 'sweatshop' here operates long ten- or twelve-hour working shifts, sometimes with forced overtime. If a worker doesn't meet her unrealistic quota, she is forced to work extra time without pay until she meets it. Workers usually earn less than a living wage, often just a dollar or two a day. Sweatshops here regularly employ underage workers, and it is common to find fourteen- or fifteen-year-old girls on an assembly line. These young women, especially in garment factories, are subject to unchecked sexual harassment and abuse by managers. Others have complained about unsafe working conditions, violence, or being searched for stolen goods.

If workers try to organize, they are often fired, or worse, their companies hire *preman* (thugs) to intimidate or beat them. In March 2001, for instance, striking workers from a car upholstery manufacturer in East Jakarta were attacked by seven busloads of hired thugs with swords, knives, and home-made bombs. Two workers were killed and ten were badly injured.

Concerns about sweatshops are commonly dismissed by company executives who say, "Well, at least we're providing jobs." Of course in the back of their minds they are thinking they can always pack up and move

TANAH ABANG

IN A LAWLESS, CORRUPT CITY, somebody has to take charge, instill public order, and demonstrate accountability. Thank God for *preman*, Jakarta's very own brand of Mafioso-like thugs. They might not have cool Italian accents, carry fat shotguns, or sit in glamorous restaurants exchanging long, drawn-out stories to illustrate a moral point or a family value. But they are Jakarta's true bosses, and nobody crosses them – especially the police, military, and municipality.

The immigrant neighborhood of Tanah Abang (see 'Melting Pot' chapter) is their heartland – the place they live, breathe and do business (or just sit out on a bench and sun their potbellies). Most of Jakarta's serious *prèman* came here from Ambon in the Maluku islands, and other parts of Indonesia's 'Wild East', like Flores and Timor.

A *preman*'s bread and butter is protection money, most often called *pungli*, short for *pungutan liar*, or 'wild tax'. The serious work is in paying friendly visits to gambling dens and brothels around the city. A day of 'doing the rounds' will garner about Rp 3 to 5 million (around $300-500) for a single *preman* gang. But a whole network of petty protection fee 'clients' exists around Tanah Abang, which is home to one of Jakarta's largest public markets. Vendors pay thugs a daily fee for the privilege of, well, existing. Cars, motorbikes and taxis pay *preman* 'traffic coordinators' a fee just to enter the area. It adds up to a hell of a lot, and control of this amazing 'natural resource' is shared these days by three main gangs: Ucu, Nidin and Barok.

The municipality has been trying to crack down on these friendly boys, and recently allocated Rp 24 billion (around $2.4 million!) and a 5600-strong anti-*preman* security 'field force', so far without results.

But Tanah Abang offers more than just smiling thugs. Its market carries everything under the sun, including textiles, colorful prayer beads, and superb, freshly ground coffee. And plenty of its inhabitants aren't *preman* at all. Some are just honest, hard-working folks trying to earn a living amidst all the chaos.

THE DARK, CAVERNOUS Tanamur disco is as much a Jakarta institution as the National Monument or National Museum, but no doubt enjoys many more visitors and a much higher revenue. Tanamur is named after the street on which it sits – Tanah Abang Timur – and has been hosting a colorful mix of clientele representing every creed, age and sexual orientation since opening its doors in 1971. The venue is notorious for its scantily clad go-go dancers who slither around poles, the high percentage of transvestites and ladies-of-the-night in its crowd, and the anything-goes atmosphere. Tanamur's own website makes no effort to hide the club's nature: "Don't be surprised to see your customer/client/boss here who three hours earlier excused themselves from going out for a nightcap after dinner because they were 'feeling tired and had a big day tomorrow'". The website even translates Indonesian expressions deemed useful inside the club. "Do you want to go back to the hotel with me?" and "Let's go back to my hotel now!" are just a few of the suggested phrases that attest to the club's wholesome, family-like environment.

The music is good, though, so many young Jakartans come here just to let loose on the dance floor. It's a curious social mix, but there's method to the madness – a kind of informal division of 'turf'. The straight crowd (and a smattering of *waria* ladyboys) generally occupies the front section of the club; gay revelers hang out on the upstairs balcony; and middle-aged expat men generally linger in the back, where veteran working girls occupy the barstools. The most famous bargirl is called 'Tits.' Hers are bigger than watermelons, and she gets the most money and speaks fluent English. Some of these ladies are in fact so 'veteran' that they're charmingly referred to as 'Tanamur furniture' and were reportedly on hand for the disco's opening some thirty years ago. Ah, history.

Next door and under the same ownership lays an institution of comparable ill repute, the long-standing JJ Duit – or JJ's. The interaction here is very straightforward, principally, white males picking up Indonesian bar girls, i.e. the prototypical urban Asian meat market. Like elsewhere in Indonesia, bar girls here are known as *ayam* ('chicken'). The music is mostly a mix of R & B and Hip-Hop, a tiny dance floor hosts pretty young things gyrating frantically at their own reflection in a wall of mirrors, and the drinks are, well, clearly not the specialty here. A second-floor balcony overlooking the dance floor has curiously become the domain of Jakarta's male African population; the courtyard outside is the place to mingle or conduct (for the truly ambitious) a conversation.

Both venues have in recent years become pet targets for Muslim fundamentalist 'morality raids', particularly during the fasting month of Ramadan, making them arguably the most exciting nightspots in town.

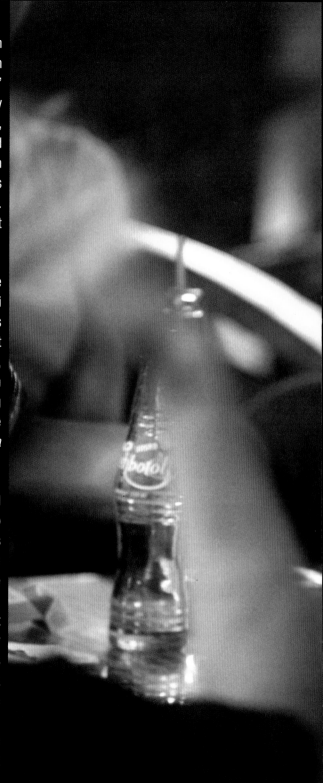

TEH BOTOL

IF THERE IS a modern-day national Indonesian beverage, surely it is *Teh Botol*, the slim brown bottles of iced tea found in street side vendors' coolers, on supermarket shelves and at family restaurants. In Jakarta's hot and humid climate, the chilled thirst-quencher is every school kid and office commuter's best friend. Even foreigners love it, because it's not quite as sugary-sweet as many other Indonesian drinks. And at just Rp 1,500 (about 15 cents) a bottle, it is affordable to just about anyone.

So popular is *Teh Botol* that just to stay in the local beverage game, the Coca-Cola and Pepsi companies ended up launching their own lines of bottled tea to hack away at local tea giant Sosro's runaway (77%!) market share. Indeed, the generic term *Teh Botol* actually comes from the brand name of Sosro's industry-leading product, but around seventeen other labels are now in the market, such as the popular *Teh Kita* and *Frestea*.

The idea of bottling iced tea apparently evolved from a mid-1960s logistical dilemma at Sosro in promoting their line of Jasmine tea. Sales agents traveled from village to village, offering samples of the stuff to crowds of prospective consumers. On-the-spot brewing took too long, however, so Sosro began preparing samples at the office and transporting ready-made tea by truck in giant pots and pans. But in those days Jakarta's roads were still so bad that the tea flew all over the back of the truck. Hence, the brilliant idea to stick the damn stuff in bottles. When Sosro introduced *Teh Botol* in 1970, it was the first known ready-to-drink bottled iced tea in the world.

TOLL ROADS

TOLL ROADS WERE OFFICIALLY touted as a magical solution to Jakarta's worsening traffic situation. But everyone knew these mega-projects were really about the magical sums of money they produced for their proud owners, the most prominent of whom just happened to be former president Soeharto's daughter, Tutut.

Toll roads are funny things, because while they were created to ease the flow of traffic, they are actually the cause of some of the worst stop-and-go gridlock in the city, with the added insult that drivers actually have to *pay* for the experience (and the added *added* insult that Tutut is not especially — how to put it? — popular these days).

It would be tempting to fire off some cliché about toll roads being "a permanent fixture of Jakarta's landscape…" (as is done about so many other subjects in this book). But in 1999, angry mobs frustrated with the results of the presidential election set fire to a number of major tollbooths, proving there was little 'permanent' or 'fixed' about them. Not only was this a potent act of symbolism by a frustrated populace against the powers that be, it also meant the public could use the toll road absolutely free for the next few days until the razed structures were rebuilt.

Additional important toll road folklore: In a popular TV commercial a few years back, a guy drives up to a tollbooth, looking like he's suffering from a bad cold. Instead of a ticket, the sweet, sympathetic female operator hands him a packet of Xon-Ce brand Vitamin C. The same driver returns day after day and when handed just a regular toll ticket, asks "Xon-Cenya mana?!" ("Where's the Xon-Ce?!"). During the period in which the ad aired, toll booth attendants endured countless cries of "Where's the Xon-Ce?!" from drivers who all thought themselves terribly funny and original. And actress Elma Theana built a career almost entirely on her timeless performance as the charming tollbooth operator. Shame that in reality most operators look more Elmer Fudd than Elma Theana.

142

TRAFFIC COPS

THESE ARE THE boys Jakarta drivers love to hate, because the smiling, tight-uniformed traffic cops are the embodiment of small-scale, everyday police corruption. Nasty habits die hard, it turns out, even in an era of much-celebrated *reformasi*.

So drivers get edgy whenever they traverse the Thamrin and Hotel Indonesia roundabouts, where traffic cops almost always lie in wait for a fresh victim…er, violator. Pass by these 'hot spots' and you'll nearly always witness a hapless driver pulled over with a befuddled "But what did I do, officer?" look upon his face. This being Indonesia, things are resolved with a swift palming of cash from driver to cop, called *uang damai* ('peace money'). The amount varies; if you drive of crappy car or manage a sufficiently desperate front while negotiating, a Rp 20,000 (around $2) bribe might do. If your car looks like it's worth more than the national defense budget, or if they happen to think you look Chinese-Indonesian (i.e. supposedly wealthy), you could get hit for Rp 50-70,000 (around $5-7). The only consistent thing about the system is that how much you pay has absolutely nothing to do with the severity of your alleged misdemeanor. Once business is settled, you go on your merry way, and the cop will pull over the next sucker.

This interaction is not surprising, because traffic cops are very poorly paid. A typical member of Jakarta's traffic police force receives a monthly salary of just Rp 600-800,000 (around $60-80) but brings home as much as Rp 4 million (around $400) in bribes. In fact, the city's traffic cops become a whole lot more diligent and work much longer hours towards the end of each month, when the previous month's salary starts wearing thin. A cop's assignment to a lucrative 'wet' (i.e. bribe-heavy) traffic spot is arranged by his superior, so the superior can expect a handsome cut from any action, and the kickbacks move steadily upward. In one small city outside Jakarta, for instance, the chief of police regularly received an estimated Rp 75 million (around $7,500) per month from his subordinate at the traffic police section.

Cocky drivers will sometimes try to bluff their way out of this predicament by dropping the name of some police chief bigwig: "I know your boss, Colonel So-And-So! He's my uncle! I'll give him a call so that he can demote you to security guard!" Frequently, the traffic cop won't risk the ire of his superior – regardless of whether he believes Colonel So-And-So exists – and will let the

perpetrator go. But if the cop calls the bluff…well, time to pull out that wallet.

THEATER UTAN KAYU, or TUK, is named for the street on which it sits, and is more than just a neighborhood theater and the hippest intellectual hangout in the city. It's a living symbol of resistance to the New Order regime's suppression of thought and creativity in the mid-1990s. When their outspoken newsmagazine, *Tempo*, was banned in 1994, a group of urban intellectual writers and editors led by Goenawan Mohamad were determined to create an alternative 'space' for free thought, open debate and various creative pursuits in literature and the arts.

Today TUK is a small but very busy cultural center offering programs that, by Jakarta standards anyway, are daring and unconventional. Its Lontar Gallery tends to exhibit wildly abstract things like installations featuring human urine flowing through tubes (apparently a profound message about authoritarian oppression – must admit I didn't understand that one too well). TUK's monthly film series is the closest thing Jakarta has to art-house cinema, with themes ranging from contemporary gay film to retrospectives on 1920s silent Norwegian horse movies (not really, but pretty much). TUK even houses a media think tank, ISAI (Institute for the Study of Free Flow of Information), which is currently studying how to shorten its name. The adjacent bookshop stocks a good selection of highbrow Indonesian literature, and is probably the only place in Jakarta that sells Che Guevera and Karl Marx t-shirts. The most important part of TUK is undoubtedly the courtyard café, where artists, journalists, thinkers and wannabe thinkers gather to chat.

Jakarta's other busy cultural center, Taman Ismail Marzuki (TIM), was a pet project of former Jakarta governor Ali Sadikin (see 'Bang Ali' chapter) and opened its doors in 1968. It is named after Ismail Marzuki, composer of patriotic independence-era Indonesian songs. According to one local guidebook, "his large bust was erected in 1984" and stands by the main entrance. Poor soul.

TIM is home to the Jakarta Institute of Arts (IKJ), as well as a great second-hand bookshop run by the eccentric poet José Rizal Manua, who also teaches drama at the center's school for street kids. TIM also houses a multiplex cinema, a large theater, two art galleries, and the Jakarta Planetarium. Like at TUK, the real 'scene' here is at the outdoor cafés. Occasional sidewalk festivals really bring this venue to life.

HALF THE YEAR is rainy season in Jakarta, when dark late-afternoon skies descend eerie and low over gleaming skyscrapers, and monsoon downpours slap relentlessly against shingled orange rooftops and slippery roads. It's a pretty romantic scene when observed through an office-building window or the tinted windshield of a Land Cruiser. But if you're caught out on the street, running late for an important meeting and temporarily trapped under the flimsy awning of a cigarette stall, you could be forgiven for thinking that life just really sucks.

Enter umbrella boys – called *tukang payung* – heroes of the hour and surely God's own little barefoot angels. They appear miraculously outside hotel and office building lobbies, near footbridges and bus stops and supermarket doors, or just about anywhere folks might require momentary cover to reach their car. Umbrella boys are young – sometimes just five or six years of age, and carry huge umbrellas that dwarf their own tiny frames. For a small fee – usually Rp 1,000 (around 10 cents) – the shivering, sniffling boys escort customers to a nearby destination, arms stretched high so that the umbrella protects their client from the rain. It is a mark of the boys' customer-is-always-dry policy that they are themselves almost always soaked through to the bone. Show me an umbrella boy who is not dripping wet and I'll expose him for the phony that he is.

Umbrella boys have arguably the most seasonally varied job on earth. Forget farmers, these boys are summoned for duty so randomly and intermittently that any notion of 'job security' needs to be placed in a whole different context. Obviously, their market peaks in the rainy period from September to March each year, but rain can sometimes appear even in the middle of Jakarta's so-called dry season, creating a sudden market niche for properly-equipped, highly alert umbrella boys.

149

URBAN LEGENDS & MYSTERY

JAKARTA – A MODERN METROPOLIS of ten million rational, enlightened residents? Not always. Throw a stone in any direction, and it's bound to hit someone who's got a supernatural tale to spin. And if they happen not to have a spooky story to relay, odds are they know someone who's heard of a guy whose cousin's deaf aunt can supposedly see jinns or ghosts. These are the people who watched *The Sixth Sense* and thought, "So the kid can see dead people…big deal!" In Jakarta, three monthly magazines dealing with the paranormal – *Misteri*, *Mistis* and *Posmo* – are currently amongst the hottest publications on the market.

It's hard to know why so many Jakartans, and Indonesians in general, are hopelessly captivated by all things mysterious. One obvious explanation is the whole link to animist beliefs, but never mind the anthro-babble, because most of my Indonesian friends haven't been animists for years. Another possibility is that day-to-day life for many Jakartans can be so disheartening that anything supernatural, however far-fetched, feels like a vast improvement. Then again, it's not just *kampung* dwellers who buy into superstitions; by many accounts former presidents Soeharto and Gus Dur relied more on spiritual counselors than political advisers – suggesting a leadership style almost as folksy and superstitious as that of…Nancy and Ronald Reagan.

Local obsession with the inexplicable is all over Jakarta's mass media: TV, radio, gossip tabloids and the internet all carry stories of reincarnation, conspiracy, ghosts and demons. Last year's *Jelangkung* – an Indonesian film about a ghost-hunting gang of kids – was a huge box office success because it hit a lot closer to home than your average Hollywood horror flick (the certain-to-be-watered-down Tinseltown re-make of *Jelangkung* is currently in development).

Ghost hunting has in fact become somewhat of a hobby in Jakarta, and its enthusiasts hang out at cemeteries hoping to catch a glimpse of a legendary spirit. Certain locations around the city are reputed to be hotspots for undead activity, like the Jeruk Purut cemetery, which features a headless preacher, and the abandoned house pictured here, located in the middle of the affluent Pondok Indah suburb (see 'Pondok Indah Houses' chapter). These places have become domestic tourist attractions of sorts, offering young Jakartans just enough spook to make a visit there more intriguing than yet another ho-hum trip to Monas Park.

IF IT WEREN'T for the thinly concealed unemployment behind the *Pak Ogah* phenomenon, watching these unofficial 'traffic regulators' pretend to direct the flow of cars, buses and motorbikes would no doubt be one of Jakarta's most amusing spectacles. Truth be told, it is anyway.

Nearly every intersection in the city – from neighborhood corners to major toll road underpasses – is marked by the scruffy, authoritative presence of a *Pak Ogah*. The term is named after a lazy, unemployed watchman in a popular early-'80s kids TV series, who wouldn't move unless someone gave him a handout. His famous refrain was *"cepek dulu dong!"* ("a hundred rupiah first!"). Which is pretty much what today's *Pak Ogah* say in between releasing deafening shrieks from their bright-colored whistles and highly-animated, mostly-meaningless gestures with their hands. 'Stingy' drivers who refuse to pay can sometimes end up with serious scratches to their car, or even a broken windshield.

What everybody knows but nobody bothers to admit is that *Pak Ogah* – by stalling vehicles mid-turn to collect a few coins from each driver – actually hinder the flow of traffic in Jakarta, which in turn creates the need for even more *Pak Ogah* to supposedly ease the flow of traffic.

Pak Ogah can expect to receive between Rp 100 to Rp 1,000 (about 1 to 10 cents) from each driver, depending on the driver's generosity or, as is often the case, the degree to which a driver might be intimidated by a particularly rough-looking *Pak Ogah*. 'Owning' a corner is of course a matter of neighborhood turf allocation – highly sensitive and carefully regulated by local mafia bosses, who normally get a cut from the daily take.

PERHAPS NO GROUP in Jakarta enjoys a higher profile relative to their small numbers than the *waria*, members of the city's ladyboy subculture.

Like trannies everywhere, Indonesia's *waria* (literally *wanita/pria*, or 'woman/man') have gravitated to the big city, acquiring a degree of anonymity not afforded by village life, and a strong, like-gendered support network. Sisters may be stepping out, sometimes realizing the dream of living full-time as women, finding a job and netting a husband. But the reality for most *waria* is a long way from a Priscilla-like acceptance by polite society. Although the authorities rarely harass them, *waria* are never really allowed to fit in, and are generally resigned to careers as entertainers or prostitutes. Many have migrated from other parts of Indonesia, so their sense of alienation is doubly felt.

Nearly all *waria* eventually drift into *mejeng*, or sex work, where they find a large client base of men on the prowl for something different. Different is what they get. Some *waria* have undergone complete sex changes, either in Indonesia of overseas, while others stay 'technically male' but undergo breast enlargement surgery, inject silicon into their faces, or take female hormones for a more voluptuous look.

High-end *waria* sex workers of the type rarely found working the streets buy make-up in fancy shopping malls, wear designer outfits from top boutiques, receive client calls on ultra-slim handphones, and take home up to Rp 500,000 (around $50) a night. More visible are the *waria* found in numbers causing late-night traffic headaches on the main drag above Lawang Park in Jakarta's leafy Menteng. Commonly referred to by the more derogatory terms, *bencong* and *banci*, they survive on a diet of taxi drivers, army officers and local businessmen.

Reality for most, however, is even more dire, turning Rp 20,000 (around $2) tricks along the railway tracks, all the while playing Russian Roulette with sexual predators and STDs of every kind. This is life on Jakarta's sidelines.

DESPITE THE UBIQUITY of handphones, laptops, and PDAs amongst Jakarta's increasingly gadget-savvy yuppie class, the economy doesn't allow most folks their own phone line or computer. So in the same manner people used to share a neighborhood water pump or a village idiot, Jakartans fall back on communal forms of access to communication technology. Nothing better exemplifies this than *wartel* and *warnet*.

A *wartel* (*warung telepon,* or 'telephone stall') is a quick, user-friendly way to phone anyone from your aunt in the next neighborhood to your spoiled cousin who's off bagging a degree in Business Admin at the University of Iowa. *Wartel* are everywhere, and they're way better than ordinary public payphones, which require a sack of coins, allow only local calls, and nearly always smell of urine. At a *wartel* you can call virtually any number, including handphone and international destinations; you can keep track of the cost via a bright red meter in the booth, and never have to deal with annoying beeps prompting you to insert more coins to keep the connection going. When you're done, just hang up, and the *wartel* operator will print out your bill from a central computer.

Then again, it's irritating when the *wartel* is packed and you're stuck behind someone with apparently way too much time and money who's trying to woo a chick on the other end. Even worse is when you're in the booth next to a loud-mouth, because the paper-thin walls make it hard to have a meaningful phone conversation amid the strains of someone loudly uttering "No, really? You're kidding!" every 30 seconds.

The logical extension of the *wartel* is the *warnet*, or *warung internet*. Often located in shopping centers, they are essentially clusters of cubicles equipped with internet-enabled PCs – in a sense the cyber-café's poorer cousin. It's a significant innovation, because it means millions of young Indonesians who could never afford their own computer can access the internet for as little as Rp 5,000 (around 50 cents) per hour. They are therefore 'technologically empowered', which means that like young people everywhere they too can waste six hours each day in mindless online chat (often with friends sitting right in the adjacent cubicle), surfing porn sites, or competing in live, multi-player shoot-'em-up games against geeky teenage counterparts in Singapore. Drawbacks? The occasional bum connections, and the *warnet* keeper's questionable taste in music when playing mp3s, ostensibly for customer enjoyment (the unfortunate *Titanic* theme springs to mind). The cubicles don't provide much privacy, either, especially when you're opening that much-anticipated e-love letter from a high school heartthrob. But *warnet* are a great example of globalization in action. Thomas L. Friedman would be proud.

157

WC. UMUM
KAMAR MA

Jakartans

in

Caricature

by Benny and Mice

Neighborhood Local

'Haji' cap, gift from neighbor who recently returned from pilgrimage to Mecca

'kretek' clove cigarette

gem ring connoisseur

wood bracelet with magical powers

tropical fish for his collection

sarong - convenient for both praying and sleeping

Political Activist

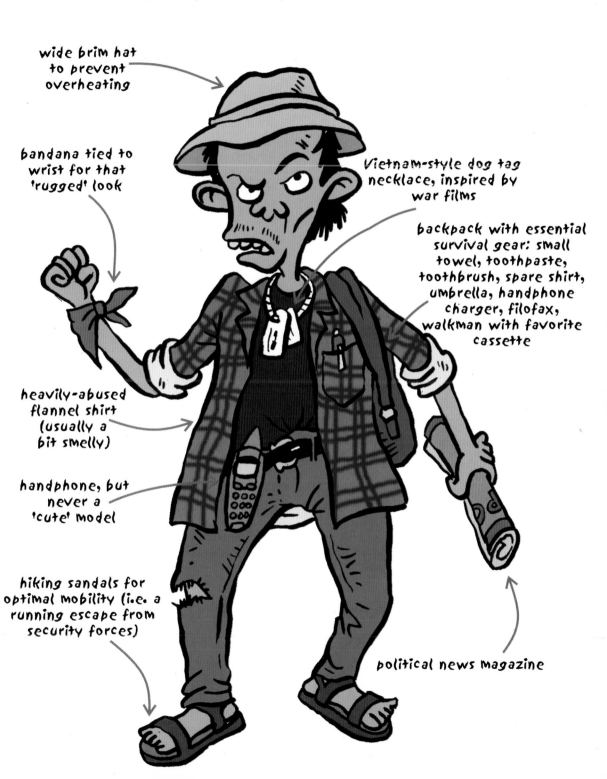

wide brim hat to prevent overheating

bandana tied to wrist for that 'rugged' look

Vietnam-style dog tag necklace, inspired by war films

backpack with essential survival gear: small towel, toothpaste, toothbrush, spare shirt, umbrella, handphone charger, filofax, walkman with favorite cassette

heavily-abused flannel shirt (usually a bit smelly)

handphone, but never a 'cute' model

hiking sandals for optimal mobility (i.e. a running escape from security forces)

political news magazine

Mall Babe

never used, just a
fashion statement

dyed hair

colored contact lenses,
matched to clothing

latest, trendiest
Nokia handphone

braces (cost 3
million rupiah)

temporary
tattoo

contents:
cash, ATM card,
credit card,
photobooth mug shot,
name card

contents:
cosmetics, tissues,
maxi-pads

panties waving
hello from
waistline

panty line, result of
ultra-tight pants

Society Lady

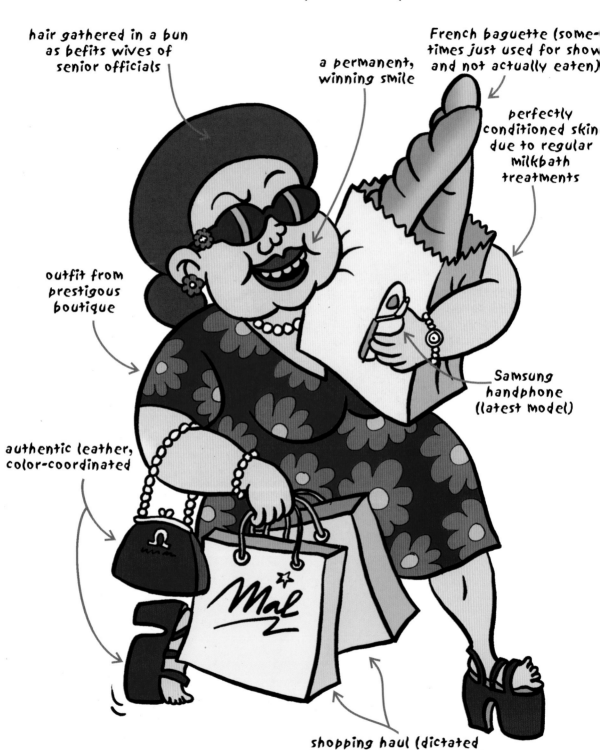

hair gathered in a bun as befits wives of senior officials

a permanent, winning smile

French baguette (sometimes just used for show and not actually eaten)

perfectly conditioned skin due to regular milkbath treatments

outfit from prestigous boutique

Samsung handphone (latest model)

authentic leather, color-coordinated

shopping haul (dictated by latest fashion trends)

Neighborhood Thug ('Preman')

Bar 'Bule'

Ladyboy Busker

TOP 10 ALTERNATIVE THINGS TO DO IN JAKARTA

Official guidebooks will tell you about Sunda Kelapa harbor, the National Museum, Old Jakarta's Fatahillah Square and the Jalan Surabaya antique market. Whatever. The REAL Jakarta lies elsewhere, so if you're tired of doing the tourist thing, or sick of those air-conditioned shopping malls, here are some ideas:

1. Japan Town

Head to the few square blocks known as Kompleks Blok M, just off Jalan Melawai and across from Blok M Plaza Mall. This delightful maze of Izakaya restaurants, Japanese specialty supermarkets and multi-floored karaoke bars is a Jakarta idiosyncrasy that never gets old.

2.Muara Karang Seafood Dining

The most adventurous dining experience in Jakarta, and possibly the most delicious. Make your way to this enormous seafood market off the docks north of Pluit (ask the taxi to stand by, as they are hard to find out there); check out the fresh fish, crabs, lobsters, prawns, mussels and stingrays; bargain hard, then take your haul to the adjacent *lesehan*-style dining stands (seating is on the floor of a raised platform); surrender your purchases to the staff, tell them what style you want your food cooked, order fresh coconut juice in the shell, and await a delicious feast.

3. A Day at the Spa

Spoiling oneself all day in a decadent spa (like Xanadu, Bimasena, Bersih Sehat or Martha Tilaar) is one of Jakarta's great treats, and can cost a tenth of the price of a similar indulgence in the West. Treatments range from traditional Indonesian and Shiatsu-style massage to facials, foot reflexology and 'mandi lulur' milk baths. Book ahead, especially on weekends.

4. Early Morning at Pasar Senen

Photo enthusiasts and early-morning wanderers will love the color and energy of this bustling market. It has just about everything, but the highlight is the dawn cake market, which supplies vendors all over town. The adjacent Senen train station is also a magical place at this early hour.

5. Kota at Night & Breakfast at Café Batavia

After dark, Jakarta's Chinatown becomes a one-stop theme park of entertainment, but not just of the seedy variety; Jalan Hayam Wuruk is home to some of the city's best food stalls and coffee stands. Restaurants like the Jayakarta and Super Kitchen serve delicious Chinese food until the wee hours. And the stunning Café Batavia, open 24 hours, is the classic place for an early morning wind-down breakfast.

6. Menteng Plaza & Late Night Street Dining

One friend called this strip "the closest thing in Jakarta to a London high street." Indeed, Menteng Plaza has everything from a supermarket to restaurants, a pharmacy, a department store, and a handful of popular bars. But its claim to fame is the variety and quality of its evening street side dining stalls, and lively atmosphere. Some great street musicians play here, and as can be seen from the numerous Mercedes and Beemers parked up against the *sate* and porridge stalls, it's a favorite drive-thru dining spot for Jakarta's young and affluent.

7. Sunday Jogging at Senayan & Jalan Sudirman

Pounding the pavement of Jakarta's main thoroughfare on Sunday mornings (closed to traffic from 6 to 9 AM) ain't exactly a jog along a pristine beach. But if you're an outdoorsy fitness type, this is about as good as it gets in this city. Join rollerbladers, cyclists and runners on Jalan Sudirman, or head to nearby Senayan stadium for similar activities plus some great roadside breakfast dim sum stalls. Amazingly, Jakarta's governor recently announced plans to ban even this small pleasure (see next page for 5 Wild & Crazy Ideas for Jakarta's Governor).

8. Weekend Buffet Brunch or Dim Sum

Jakarta's decadent weekend brunches will leave you so happy, stuffed and useless that they should never be attempted if you need to function in any way later on in the afternoon. Most are at luxury hotels and include specialty corners for seafood, sushi and roasts. Arrive on a very empty stomach and expect to pay from Rp 90,000 to 200,000 (around $9-20) per head for an all-you-can-eat feast to die for. At the time of writing, best bets were: Margaux at the Shangri-La Hotel (pricey but very classy), Il Mare at the Mulia Senayan Hotel (mostly Italian), Seasons at The Regent (the biggest by far), and Paprika restaurant (Sundays only). A dim sum outing will set you back even less, and places like Ming, Crystal Jade, Dragon City, Samudra and Ah Yat Abalone dish out cuisine on par with some of the best establishments in Asia.

9. Glodok (Chinatown) Market & Temples

This is Jakarta at its most ornamental and exotic, but also at its most genuine. No other neighborhood in the city boasts such a distinctive vibe, so when you're feeling like the city is one big concrete bore, head for this semi-covered market and take in its many delights. Stop for a hearty bowl of noodle dumpling soup, then find the entrance to narrow Petak Sembilan alleyway. It leads you past a small seafood market where they're often skinning frogs, and on to two of the most beautiful Taoist/Buddhist *klenteng* (temples) in the city. The light here is gorgeous in late afternoon. When on the brink of heat exhaustion, retreat to the air-con of nearby Mangga Dua Mall and check out the bargain electronics.

10. TUK & TIM

Jakarta isn't Tokyo or Sydney when it comes to the arts, but there's still plenty going on, and some of it can be very cutting-edge and worthwhile. Teater Utan Kayu (TUK) in East Jakarta, and Taman Ismail Marzuki (TIM) in Central Jakarta's Cikini district are almost always up to something new and interesting, whether in dance, music, experimental theater, film or art. For current listings check *djakarta! – The City Life Magazine*, *The Jakarta Post*, *Jakarta Kini* or the cultural journal *Aikon*.

5 WILD AND CRAZY IDEAS
FOR
JAKARTA'S GOVERNOR

1. Stop demolishing people's homes.

Whether or not these penniless slum-dwellers have housing 'permits' from greedy, corrupt municipal officials living in Menteng mansions is entirely irrelevant. They are human beings, and as such should enjoy the basic right to a roof over their heads, which is something the municipality itself has done nothing to provide. If you must tear down a slum and uproot people from their homes, make sure you offer alternative housing, meaning not just better dwellings but schools, jobs, sanitation and security for the urban refugees you so effortlessly create. And don't ever say that they shouldn't have settled in these places in the first place. It's demeaning both to them and to the office you hold.

2. Impose and rigorously enforce smog control on buses.

Jakarta's appalling pollution has many sources, but surely the most scandalous must be the thick clouds of black smoke from the huge buses that ply our roads. When your traffic cops are not busy pulling over innocent motorists and hitting them for bribes, have them pull over buses that fail to meet emission standards, and ground these vehicles. Meeting these standards will be costly to bus companies, but that is exactly who should pay the price for pollution, not the public. Introducing and enforcing smog control would also create a huge industry for fixing and testing smog emission, surely a welcome development for garage owners or the unemployed. Oh – and stop doing this as a cynical, one-off photo-op on annual Earth Day, because it looks (and is) ridiculous. If you crack down on buses and pollution as forcefully and consistently as you evict slum-dwellers, the difference in air quality will be felt within weeks.

3. Re-prioritize the municipal budget so that it reflects the REAL needs of the city.

This means the allocation for poverty alleviation should probably exceed the budget for luxury private cars given to council members. Similarly, city councilors' "study trips" to Tokyo and New York would best be replaced by study trips to Kramat and Cilincing so that something relevant to their job is actually learned in the process. And hey – they would actually get to meet real people with real problems, although admittedly this could be unpleasant.

4. Recognize Jakarta's heritage treasures.

Restore, revive and maintain them. For all the official rhetoric in City Tourism Promotion Board brochures, let's be honest – Jakarta currently offers very little to prospective visitors. If you must go on an overseas 'study tour' this year (and no doubt you will), head for Singapore, and witness what they've done with Clark and Boat Quays, their colonial district, their markets, their museums. Yes, this all costs money, but Gov, YOU HAVE MONEY. You know you do. It's just drowning in a sea of corruption and ineptitude. Salvage it and use it. Drive up to Old Kota and look around you. With a small dose of planning and commitment 'Colonial' Jakarta can be transformed into a world-class attraction that would lure not only tourists but also businesses. See all those old buildings? Stop tearing them down! They are key! Fix the traffic mess that leads to this quarter. Install lighting and labeling and air-conditioning in Kota's museums. Discuss tax breaks – not kickbacks – with heritage developers. Clean out and illuminate Kali Besar so it becomes a picturesque canal rather than the foul-smelling eyesore that it is today.

5. Create 'lungs' for the city.

This one is very basic. Monas, Jakarta's largest park, could easily be turned into a truly public, green oasis where people can breathe, exercise and contemplate their urban existence. Problem is, you've placed too many soldiers, policemen and guards there for anyone to feel relaxed or enjoy themselves, unless the idea was to create a New Order theme park. You allow traffic to choke the air, and for all the 'troops' stationed there, the place still doesn't feel secure at night. Money spent on the enforcement of meaningless rules and underemployed soldiers could be diverted to really making the place green. Trees – a radical concept. Lush expanses of grass – pricey, but probably not as costly as your personal monthly housing allowance. You could even create a regulated area for food vendors rather than always chasing them away. Oh, and an open-air stage, and proper lighting to make the whole place safe. Is this too much to ask? One such park in the entire city? One?

RECOMMENDED ENGLISH-LANGUAGE RESOURCES ON JAKARTA

BOOKS

The Jakarta Explorer: Cultural Tours In and Around the City
by The Indonesian Heritage Society
A must for local culture enthusiasts, and thus far the best guide to Jakarta's many sites, from the obvious to the obscure. Practical information, historical background, and cultural insights on some of the city's most interesting spots. Available through the Heritage Society, tel. 572-5870.

Batavia in 19th-Century Photographs
by Scott Merrillees
An impressive collection of rare photos from Jakarta's former life as Dutch-colonial 'Batavia'. Well researched and beautifully presented.

Tales From Djakarta
by Pramoedya Ananta Toer
Thirteen short stories set in 1940s and 1950s Jakarta by Indonesia's most celebrated writer. Pram delivers these intriguing tales with his trademark honesty and acute sense of place.

The Year of Living Dangerously
by Christopher Koch
An evocative reconstruction of a city on the brink of political disaster during the chaotic final month's of Sukarno's rule. The 1980s Hollywood adaptation starring Mel Gibson didn't do justice to Koch's lyrical prose.

Twilight in Djakarta
by Mochtar Lubis
This powerful novel describes the plight of the poor in 1950s Jakarta, and is a scathing attack on corruption. It's a classic book that's been on and off the ban list in Indonesia for a while.

The Jakarta Good Food Guide
by Laksmi Pamuntjak
A comprehensive, beautifully-written guide to the city's dining spots, from up-market bistros and buffets to roadside porridge stalls. This user-friendly resource includes hundreds of critical reviews – a must for everyone from the casual diner to the seasoned culinary connoisseur.

WEB

www.expat.or.id – Living in Indonesia: A Site for Expatriates
One of the best online sources of general information on living in Jakarta and Indonesia. Includes a wealth of practical information on the city, articles on local culture, a directory of community organizations and excellent web links.

MEDIA

djakarta! – The City Life Magazine
The capital's most comprehensive city mag is a bilingual, one-stop source for practical information on everything going on in town. This independent, alternative monthly carries critical reviews and previews of events, in-depth features on city issues and great photography.

The Jakarta Post
The city's only English-language daily contains a good mix of local, national and international news, and has earned a reputation as one of the most critical and unbiased publications in Indonesia.

Latitudes Magazine
A smart, insightful cultural monthly based in Bali but covering the entire archipelago, including plenty of in-depth, refreshing material on Jakarta.

MAPS

Jakarta Street Directory
by Periplus Editions
Compact, colorful directory to the city with particular attention to landmarks such as universities, markets, museums and major office buildings.

Jakarta/Jabotabek Street Atlas (a.k.a. the Falk Plan)
by Günther W. Holtorf
Easily the most comprehensive atlas to Jakarta with impressive detail and an easy-to-use layout. Includes all of Jakarta's outlying towns. Very good referencing system, and extremely up-to-date.

ACKNOWLEDGEMENTS

This book is the product of four fascinating years of watching Jakarta – initially from the outside in, and later, at least to some degree, from the inside out. Hundreds of hours of so-called barefoot empiricism (mostly pacing the streets in very odd corners of the city at very odd hours of the day and night) went a long way in acquainting me with Jakarta at ground level. But it was the people I have been privileged to know who made sense of everything in the end. The length of this acknowledgements section reflects not just my annoying tendency to overwrite, but also the great number of people to whom I am truly indebted.

Nobody influenced my understanding of Jakarta more than my insane staff at *djakarta! -The City Life Magazine*. They taught me about everything in this city from fringe culture to pop culture to high culture, introduced me to some of the strangest folks in town, and forced me to master gutter Indonesian purely for the sake their own amusement. They mocked me in the office, abused me on live radio call-in programs, and brought me to the brink of mental breakdown more often than I care to admit. But they were also the most wonderful thing to have happened to me here. To my experiences with them and through them, I owe this book. In particular, I wish to thank Mia Amalia, Helly Minarti, Toto Prastowo, Untung H.Bimo, Gaman Kamajaya, Rosa Hasan, Ening Nurjanah, Leilie Huzaibah, Pak Ahmad Jufri, Ve Handojo, Bunga D. Prihanto, Mas Purwanto, Deny, Edy Purnomo, Swanti, Widi, Timur Angin, Paul Dillon, Hasief Ardiasyah, Heru Satmoko, Sarah Cakrawati, Ima Mangiri, Meike Rumambi, Joseph T., Roy Rubianto, Camilla Adindamaulani, Muh 'Mice' Misrad, Benny Rachmadi, Zinnia Nizar, Ade Fitria Sechan, Irawaty Sarah, Mas Heri, Mas Hendro, Pak Memi, Mas Priyo and Mas Marjuki. My publishing partners at *djakarta!*, Dr Mohamed 'Kiki' Ganie and Mr Satish Mahtani, had the confidence to turn a strange idea into wonderful reality, and somehow tolerated my unconventional ways. Together we created something meaningful, innovative and daring, and I will always be grateful to them for the opportunity and experience.

In Mark Hanusz I found not just a great publisher, but also a resourceful, enthusiastic partner who poured his heart and boundless energy into this book and kept me on track in all sorts of ways. He believed in this odd project from the start and was a constant joy to work with. In between chasing photos, he somehow found time to do all the design work on this book. Mark's countless suggestions and his creative touch ended up shaping much of what is now, for better or for worse, *Jakarta Inside Out*, although I'll probably be the one to shoulder all the blame.

Sasa Kralj has been not just a mentor, teacher, friend and late-night swimming buddy, but the single human force that preserved my sanity here through all kinds of ups and downs. His love, infinite wisdom and sound advice made this book possible – as well as just about everything else I've been up to in this city. It's also been an unusual privilege to have someone of Sasa's professional caliber on board as this book's photo editor. The time and care he put into this project made all the difference in the world.

Laksmi Pamuntjak, undoubtedly Indonesia's most promising English-language writer and a very dear friend, offered support throughout and literally held my hand as I hammered out the first few tasteless chapters. Oren Murphy (and as many as eleven of his vintage cameras) joined me on early morning photo shoots, but it was his steadfast friendship and contagious humor that helped keep me afloat in this mad city. He also contributed thoughtful suggestions to an early draft. Andari Karina Anom faced the unenviable task of handling the often-obscure background research for this book under tight deadlines. She met the challenge calmly and professionally, and provided great material with an imaginative personal touch. Mbak Nanis at Equinox was always on hand to help out, making life a whole lot easier for all of us.

Some of Jakarta's finest photographers contributed images to this project, and I feel honored to have them as friends and colleagues. Sinartus Sosrodjojo and his JiwaFoto agency labored hard with Edy Purnomo, Josh Estey, Deny, Dimas Ardian, Sasa Kralj, Timur Angin and Roy Rubianto to provide terrific images. Tatan Syuflana and Achmad Ibrahim contributed great shots of their own. Mila and Dian at Arsip Majalah Tempo always found time to assist in the hunt for elusive images. Benny and Mice's excellent cartoon art and signature humor helped to further lighten up the book.

Su Lin Lewis, Emma Woodhouse, Jeremy Wagstaff and Paul Dillon shared the crucial and surely unpleasant task of editing all this nonsense. They did their best to clean up my mess, and I'm grateful. Lely Djuhari did a chunk of early research for the book, and dug up stuff others would never have thought of. Her friendship, support, and insight made a big difference to this project. Other wonderful friends were on hand to help out with specific chapters. Hasief Ardiasyah contributed significantly to the sections on Handphones, Metro Mini, Pigeon Racing, Traffic Cops, Urban Legends and Wartel; Emma Woodhouse added her worrying thoughts on Jalan Jaksa and Macet; Kathy Petite helped out with Gay and Love Hotels. Neha Misra did the same for Sweatshops. S. and A. provided important background on Kota Nightlife. Selamat Abdul Aziz let us abuse his *gerobak es cendol* for the cover; Chisato Hara came on board to produce the launch.

Corporate sponsors are often totally disinterested parties that buy into projects as an afterthought. Ours were of a totally different breed. Aksara Bookstore, QB World Books, Plaza Senayan and Paprika Restaurant & Wine Lounge supported this book almost unconditionally since its conception, showed keen interest in its development, and offered regular advice and support. *Jakarta Inside Out* would not have been possible without their generosity.

Richard Oh – certified madman and Godfather of Jakarta's book scene – provided contagious enthusiasm, unconditional friendship and brotherly advice throughout. Dewi "Dee" Lestari opened my eyes to what was possible here in the creative world – in literature, music and even on the home shopping channel. Her perspective and companionship have been a regular source of inspiration. P.D. 'Ndari' Prabandari and Margot Cohen – kick-ass journalists and two of my earliest friends here – showed me the ropes when all was still a bundle of confusion.

Uri Tadmor, Frank Feulner, Sergio de Rinaldini, and Susanti were not just wonderful neighbors but true friends and a surrogate family in whose company I always found comfort and encouragement. Rayya Makarim –

master scriptwriter and friend extraordinaire – helped with assorted cross-cultural insights, all kinds of trivia, and a superb writing sanctuary up in Puncak. Chris Brummitt offered shocking commentary on just about everything we encountered together, thus single-handedly making this city seem a more colorful place. *He* really should have written this book, and the influence of his signature tastelessness is doubtless felt throughout. He rides a green Ninja motorbike, and I promised him I'd mention that here. Guy Sharett, soul mate and constant source of inspiration, similarly revealed to me unique angles of the city and its people, and personally extended the limits of just of how far a foreigner can become immersed in local nuance. Nataya Aryadni provided valuable help with the early design for this book. Her ideas and enthusiasm helped shape this product. Scott Merrillees, author of the excellent *Batavia in 19th-Century Photographs*, offered early encouragement and generous advice. Dave, Barb, Jason and Cary provided a great place to write while in Vancouver. Josh Kreger kept me sane during the final push in Jakarta. Mbak Yanti has been not only a great housekeeper but also a cheerful, caring presence in my life in Jakarta and an enthusiastic partner for early-morning strolls through Slipi. These past few years would not have been the same without her help, dedication and friendship.

Many other great friends provided support, encouragement and companionship during the work on this book. While I'm undoubtedly forgetting a few, I know I am indebted in all sorts of ways to Jason Tedjasukmana, Charlie Dharapak, Dini Djalal, Jeremy Gross, Hanaa Makarim, Wimar Witoelar, Marco Kusumawijaya, Daniel Cooney, Dian Saputra, Kathleen Reen, DY Suharya, Adey Noor, Tom Wright, Mark Nelson, Shanty Harmayn, Alice Joe, Ichiki-San, Ayu Utami, William Wongso, Seno Gumira Ajidarma, Pramoedya Ananta Toer, Dewi Watson, Swanti, Oscar Lawalata, Winfred Hutabarat, Goenawan Mohamad, 'Uncle JC' Falch, Irawati Dewi, John McGlynn, Degung Santikarma, Tam Notosusanto, John Sidel, Andrea Woodhouse, Imelda Rosalin, Huey Attwater, Meidina Halimah, Andy and Sandy at Paprika, Anne Gouyon, Adrian Darmono, Shawnee Puti, Ade Fathia Syarif, Om Nono & Tante Tika Makarim, Gita Widya Laksmini, Keke Tubuan, Esty Sutyoko, Juliana Wilson, Jihan Labetubun, Claire Smith, Nona Zicherman, Wendi Ruky, Danielle Surkatty, Vaudine England, my new operators, colleagues and friends at DAI/OTI, Joel Tesoro, Priscilla Hon, Diarmid O'Sullivan, Amelia Ardan, Atika Shubert, Sari Aziz, Phil Carroll, John Long, Ed Pressman, Simon Montlake, Natacha Devillers, Jajang Pamoentjak, Natalie Amar, Jeffery Hadler Sawada, Tom McCawley, Jan Bach, Indraneel Datta, Ulrich Kratz, Sophie Joy Mosko, Patrick Rehm, Yossi Klein Halevi, Michael Oren, Eytan & Osnat & family, Mbak Dani, Mas Ipunk & Jordan.

My sisters Elana and Nomi, brother-in-law Claudio, grandmother Ida and late grandfather Morris have always been my coolest friends and most loving, enthusiastic supporters. They variously shared and shaped my passion for travel and discovery, and provided tremendous inspiration for this book.

My greatest debt is to my parents, who many years ago planted the travel bug deep inside me and are now forced to watch with mild horror and reluctant amusement as I hop from one unlikely place to the next. They instilled in me a fascination with foreign places, they taught me to observe, they taught me to write, and they taught me to think I was funny. In all of these ways and perhaps a few more, this book is entirely their fault.

POST-ACKNOWLEDGEMENTS CONFESSION

An important confession must be confessed here regarding the idea for this book, which in part I shamelessly stole from Canadian author Douglas Coupland, yes, he of *Generation-X* fame. Many people do not know that in his spare time, somewhere in between writing *Miss Wyoming* and *All Families Are Psychotic*, Douglas wrote a very excellent book called *City of Glass: Douglas Coupland's Vancouver*. As its title suggests, it is about Vancouver. Indeed, the title stands out because it includes both the book's subject and the name of its author – very resourceful. I do not know Douglas, so not only have I stolen the concept of his book, I have also, without even realizing it, somehow mustered up the nerve to refer to him on a first name basis. Douglas. Hi Douglas.

But there's more to this particular story. Shortly before our close friend Douglas became Douglas Coupland Hip Author and Pop Culture Term-Coiner for the Nineties, he worked at something else. And the something else at which he worked happened to be as a designer for a baby crib manufacturing company in Vancouver. And that baby crib manufacturing company in Vancouver, which was called Stork Craft, happened to be owned and run by my late grandfather, may he rest in peace, and my uncle. So you see, while I've never met Douglas, coincidence or historical accident mean I enjoy the kind of moral access to him that absolutely nobody, other than myself and maybe Doug, can fully understand. Whether or not this makes it ok for me to rip off his book idea is a different matter altogether. But I figure the least I can do here is come clean and tell the truth about what brings me and the Dougster together, about what underlies our exceptional, heartwarming friendship. Thanks a bunch, Douglas. I'll be mailing you a copy of this book.

PHOTO CREDITS

with kind support from

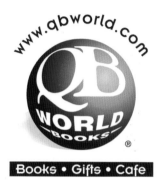

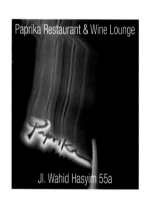